Gospel Medicine

Gospel Medicine

Barbara Brown Taylor

COWLEY PUBLICATIONS
Cambridge ✦ Boston
Massachusetts

Library of Congress Cataloging in Publication Data:
Taylor, Barbara Brown.
  Gospel medicine / Barbara Brown Taylor.
      p.   cm.
  ISBN 1-56101-110-X (alk. paper)
  1. Sermons, American—Women authors. 2. Episcopal Church—Sermons.
  3. Anglican Communion—Sermons.   I. Title.
BX5937.T28G67   1995
252'.03—dc20   94-42596
                                                          CIP

Scripture references are taken from the *New Revised Standard Version* of the Bible.

Gospel Medicine was edited by Cynthia Shattuck and designed by Vicki Black. The cover illustration is from a border decoration in the *Kalmancsehi Breviary*, Budapest.

This book is printed on recycled, acid-free paper and was produced in the United States of America.

Cowley Publications
28 Temple Place
Boston, Massachusetts 02111

For my godchildren
Patrick, Madeline, and Zachary,
my nephew Will,
and for the world they inherit.

Table of Contents

Foreword

THE WORLD TURNS and conflict flares up like a struck match. A soccer field fills with fresh graves. Believers are shot dead at their prayers. A thin buzzard waits three yards from a thinner child. Every tragedy deepens the question: what is the good news, exactly? Is anyone still listening?

All it takes is one day's headlines to make me wish I had gone into a more practical line of work. I would like to know how to close a wound or set a bone. I would like to land an airplane full of rice and chickens in the middle of the Sudan. I would settle for knowing how to fix a broken well pump. But no, I am a preacher—a public speaker of the gospel—and the story is all I have.

Several years ago I was busy with Luke the physician, imagining what it must have been like for him to leave his medical practice for the preaching life. The way I figure it, he did not stop carrying his black bag. He simply repacked it, taking out the scissors, scalpel, and tincture of iodine to make room for the medicine of the gospel—those healing stories of God that did more to put people back together than all the potions in the world. There were beatitudes for the stricken and prophecies for the blind. There were instructions for the paralyzed and parables for the hard of hearing. There were acted-out words of God for those who no longer trusted words and there was silence when all else had failed. Altogether it was quite an apothecary.

And not just then but now. And not just me but you. We are all doctors of the gospel. We are all tellers of the story, which does not heal by taking away the pain but by giving us a way to live with it—naming it, sharing it, enduring it. To run from what hurts is natural. To face it is not, and yet that is where our true health lies. If we are able to turn toward the pain of the world and let it do its work, the result may be hearts broken open to God and one another. Those who lose their lives shall find them.

The pages that follow do not pretend a cure. They address some of the more common ailments of our times, in the vernacular of the middle class where so many of us live. Anger, abandonment, and apocalypse are here. So are God's promises, messengers, and tender mercies. Most lives contain some of each, although few of us have words to describe them. That is why we need gospel balm. Smearing it over the skin of our days, we may begin to warm to the stories that still describe us, stories that know us better than we know ourselves. Their strength mends our weakness. Their truth thaws our falseness. Their life disinfects our death. Hearing them and telling them, we surrender ourselves to the Physician who heals us with words, dressing our wounds by stitching the raw edges of our lives to his.

One problem with practicing this kind of medicine is that it is hard to be original. Some of the remedies are handed down from generation to generation. Others are shared by friends and others stolen from who-remembers-where. Like other kinds of healing, preaching is a borrowed art that none of us does alone. I am grateful to Walter Brueggemann and Fred Craddock for their particular genius at opening scripture, to Frederick Buechner for his brilliant work on Jacob, to my editor Cynthia Shattuck for her powers of discernment, and to the people of Grace-Calvary Church for their loving support. Above all I am grateful to Ed Taylor, my nearest neighbor, whose companionship guards my own soul's health.

— *Barbara Brown Taylor*
Clarkesville, Georgia

Healing

Gospel Medicine

The spirit of the Lord is upon me, because he has anointed me to bring good news to the poor. He has sent me to proclaim release to the captives and recovery of sight to the blind, to let the oppressed go free, to proclaim the year of the Lord's favor. (Luke 4:18-19)

LUKE WAS, ACCORDING to tradition, a physician. The doctors among us know some things about him that the rest of us do not. They know how he spent his days and nights moving among people whose lives depended on him, and they know both his joy when he saved one of them and his sorrow when he did not. They know how his knowledge and skill seemed miraculous to him one moment and worthless the next. They know how wonderful it is to take part in someone's healing and how awful it is when healing does not occur. They know all that and more about Luke the physician.

But those of us who have been baptized know something else about Luke, something deeper and more fundamental about him than his life as a physician. What we know has to do with his life as a believer, a follower—a dreamer of God's dreams and a partner in God's work. We know that Luke thrived on a mystery greater than life and death, success and failure, joy and sorrow, namely: the good news that God has become one of us and that however bleak things may look to us at any given time, life will never be the same—life will never finally be lost—again.

We remember Luke as a physician but the plain fact is that once he had been baptized—like us—into the body of Christ, he assumed a new identity. While he may have con-

3

tinued to practice medicine, chances are that when he filled out a form and came to the line that said "occupation," he did not put "physician," but "disciple."

That is why we know Luke at all; not because he was a physician but because he was a disciple and a gospel writer, one of the four upon whom we depend for the good news of God's life among us. Without Luke, we would never have heard young Mary singing the *Magnificat* or old Simeon saying the *Nunc Dimittis* to the fresh baby in his arms. We would never have heard about John the Baptist's birth or the shepherds keeping watch over their flocks by night. We would know nothing about the parables of the Good Samaritan or the Prodigal Son, because they are stories that only Luke tells—Luke, whom the church remembers because he set down in writing the good news he had heard so that we could hear it in our own time, and be healed by it, and saved.

I like to think that Luke never resigned his job as a healer. He just changed medicines. Instead of prescribing herbs and spices, hot compresses and bed rest, he told stories with power to mend broken lives and revive faint hearts. Instead of pills and potions, he carried words in his black bag, words like "Weep no more," "Do not be afraid," "Your sins are forgiven," "Stand up and walk." His medicine was gospel medicine, which was Jesus' medicine—medicine that works, strangely enough, through words.

That is easy to miss, in the powerful gospel for Saint Luke's day: that Jesus' ministry with the poor, the prisoners, the blind and broken victims is first and foremost a ministry of *words*. Jesus has been anointed to *preach*, to *proclaim* the good news of release, recovery, sight, liberty. He will, incidentally, do those things before he is through, but from the beginning his ministry is not a ministry of doing but a ministry of *saying*—what God has done, what God is doing, what God will do. Everything that happens in Jesus' ministry happens after that proclamation and because of it, because the speaking of God's word is how the world began and how it goes on beginning, nourished and healed and strengthened by the strong medicine of the gospel.

Luke knew that. He knew the power of God's word, but only because he had heard about Jesus, and having heard about him, he knew that there was a whole world waiting to hear about him too. So he took his place in the long line of the servants of the word, gathering up the stories he had heard and setting them down in writing so that parents could tell them to their children and teachers to their students, so that friends could tell strangers and those who were nearby could tell those who were far off, so that others could tell others who told others until everyone, finally, had heard the good news of God in Christ.

And isn't it true? As unlikely as that crazy scheme sounds, isn't it true that everyone of us arrived at faith because someone told someone who told someone who told us? Maybe all someone said was, "Come to church with me," or "God bless you," or "Do you mind if I remember you when I pray?" In any case, chances are that each of us arrived at faith because someone said something to us—something that soothed us, or angered us, or intrigued us; something that brought us back for more. That is how it has been working for almost two thousand years. That is how a Galilean who spent his entire life in a country no bigger than New Jersey became known around the world—and all because people talk.

People talk, and word gets around. People talk, and lives change. People talk, and other people are made whole. There is a word for this age-old process that I have been reluctant to use, because it tends to make the hair stand up on the back of shy people's necks, but it is a word that has everything to do with the healing business that Luke was in.

The word, of course, is evangelism. Maybe you are not as sensitive to the word as I am, but then again, maybe you did not watch Oral Roberts on television in the early fifties like I did. I was about five when I discovered his program one Sunday morning and after that I was hooked. I never missed a show, but I kept the volume very low because my parents were not churchgoers and I was afraid they would not let me watch if they found out what I was doing.

Or, worse yet, if they found out what Oral was doing. He absolutely terrified me. The setting was always the same: a large tent somewhere in the midwest, with sawdust on the ground and people in overalls and flowered dresses sitting on benches, all of them watching Oral as he shouted into his hand-held microphone, crouching over it one minute and flinging his arms out the next, waving his sweaty handkerchief in the air. His white shirtsleeves were rolled up to his elbows and it always seemed to me that his dark suspenders served the purpose of holding him together, like packing tape, so that he did not explode right there in front of everyone.

He shouted until he was hoarse, and then he invited all those in need of healing to come forward while someone played "Just As I Am" on an electric organ. You know what happened next. One by one, the sick people in the crowd took their turns in front of him, tears streaming down their faces. First he would grip their heads in his big hands and press them in what looked like a painful way as he prayed out loud and then, so suddenly that he scared me every time, he would shout, "Heal!" and the people would rocket backward with dazed looks on their faces, to be caught and led away by someone on Oral's payroll who would certify their cure.

When I found out that Oral was an evangelist, I prayed I would never meet one in person and vowed to run for my life if I did. The trauma apparently runs deep, because not too long ago someone said he thought I was an evangelical preacher and I said, "I am not!" as if he had accused me of armed assault.

"I meant it as a compliment," he said. "It means someone who preaches good news."

"Oh," I said. "I *like* that."

Evangelist: a preacher of good news, a bearer of glad tidings, a practitioner of gospel medicine. Luke was an evangelist. He heard stories with power to heal in them and he repeated them, recorded them, so that they would be told again and again and again. But he is not the only one called to that ministry. In the Episcopal Church, every time someone is baptized in our midst we renew our own baptismal covenants, promising that we will be evangelists, too.

"Will you proclaim by word and example the Good News of God in Christ?" That is what each one of us is asked. "I will, with God's help," we answer, joining ranks with Luke and Oral Roberts, with Dietrich Bonhoeffer and Billy Graham, with Gerard Manley Hopkins and Madeleine L'Engle and Oscar Romero and Johann Sebastian Bach, with the man on the street corner who wears the sign around his neck that says, "Repent and be Saved," and with the housekeeper who tells Bible stories to the children in her care while she does the ironing.

There are a million ways to proclaim the good news, and we sell God short when we forget that, when we try to force ourselves into a narrow mold or fall silent because we cannot. Every now and then we may be called upon to stand up in some public place and give account for the hope that is in us, but nine times out of ten our evangelism will be the quiet kind: reading psalms to a sick friend, telling the truth to someone who has asked for it, ending a quarrel with words of forgiveness, writing a note that restores hope, listening to an old woman's story, laughing at a young boy's joke, inviting a stranger to come in—those are all proclamations of the good news, and if we are ever stuck for ideas we can remember all the ways good news has come to us, all the ways the medicine of the gospel has brought about our own healing.

The wonderful thing about gospel medicine is that it works right away; it is no sooner said than done, because the good news *effects* what it *proclaims.* "You are my beloved son," God says, and that is that. That is true, even when the beloved son is hanging on a cross. "Blessed are the poor," Jesus says, and that is true, even though they have no more today than they did yesterday. "You are the light of the world," he says, and we are, even when we are feeling decidedly dim, because the word of God does not come back empty. It accomplishes what it proclaims, however things may happen to look at the time.

On the one hand, the gospel is just a bunch of words: "Weep no more," "Do not be afraid," "Your sins are forgiven," "Stand up and walk." They are just words, and prescribing them to an ailing world seems as futile as putting a bandage on a broken bone or an aspirin in the hand of someone who is dying. But when we proclaim these words as *gospel*, we say more: we say that they are words that belong to someone, and that every time we speak them someone is present, speaking them with us, speaking them through us, so that we never speak them alone, and they never come back empty. They effect what they proclaim: they dry tears, they quench fears, they forgive sins, they heal souls, they make true the good news of God in Christ every time we speak them.

Every time we do, we take our places in the ancient relay of the faith, passing on the glad tidings we ourselves have heard from our predecessors in the practice of gospel medicine. May the God who has given us the will to do this thing give us the grace and power to perform it, restoring the world to health one blessed word at a time, if need be, until the whole world can join us in saying, "Amen."

Arthritis of the Spirit

Then Peter came and said to him, "Lord, if another member of the church sins against me, how often should I forgive? As many as seven times?" Jesus said to him, "Not seven times, but, I tell you, seventy-seven times." (Matthew 18:21-22)

IN CASE YOU have not noticed, Christianity is a religion in which the sinners have all the advantages. They can step on your feet fifty times and you are supposed to keep smiling. They can talk bad about you every time you leave the room and it is your job to excuse them with no thought of getting even. The burden is on you, because you have been forgiven yourself, and God expects you to do unto others as God has done unto you.

This is not a bad motivation for learning how to forgive. If God is willing to stay with me in spite of my meanness, my weakness, my stubborn self-righteousness, then who am I to hold those same things against someone else? Better I should confess my own sins than keep track of yours, only it is hard to stay focused on my shortcomings. I would so much rather stay focused on yours, especially when they are hurtful to me.

Staying angry with you is how I protect myself from you. Refusing to forgive you is not only how I punish you; it is also how I keep you from getting close enough to hurt me again, and nine times out of ten it works, only there is a serious side effect. It is called bitterness, and it can do terrible things to the human body and soul.

Last week on a trip into Atlanta I stopped at a gift shop to buy a couple of wedding presents, some nice brass picture frames, which I asked the clerk to wrap. "Well, who are they for?" she snarled. "Are you going to tell me or am I supposed to guess?" I looked at her then for the first time and saw a heavy, middle-aged woman whose brow was all bunched up over two hard, cold eyes. Her mouth turned down at the sides like she had just tasted something rancid and she had both her hands planted on the glass counter, leaning against it with such malice that I thought she might push it over on me if I irritated her any further.

Generally speaking, I get mad when someone comes at me like that, but this time I just got scared, because I could see what her anger had done to her and I wanted to get away from it before it did something similar to me. Actually, it was something stronger than plain anger that had twisted that woman's face. All by itself, anger is not that damaging. It is not much more than that quick rush of adrenaline you feel when you are being threatened. It tells you that something you hold dear is in danger—your property, your beliefs, your physical safety. I think of anger as a kind of flashing yellow light. "Caution," it says, "something is going on here. Slow down and see if you can figure out what it is."

When I do slow down, I can usually learn something from my anger, and if I am lucky I can use the energy of it to push for change in myself or in my relationships with others. Often I can see my own part in what I am angry about, and that helps, because if I had a hand in it then I can concentrate on getting my hand back out of it again instead of spinning my wheels in blame. I can, in other words, figure out what my anger has to teach me and then let it go, but when my anger goes on and on without my learning or changing anything then it is not plain anger anymore. It has become bitterness instead. It has become resentment, which a friend of mine calls "arthritis of the spirit."

So there is another motivation for learning how to forgive—not only because we owe it to God but because we owe it to ourselves. Because resentment deforms us. Because unforgiveness is a boomerang. We use it to protect ourselves—to hurt back before we can be hurt again—but it has a sinister way of circling right back at us so that we become the victims of our own ill will.

One summer the *New York Times Book Review* ran a series on the deadly sins. Joyce Carol Oates wrote on despair, Gore Vidal wrote on pride, and John Updike, of all people, wrote on lust. Mary Gordon's essay on anger was a real beauty, chiefly because she was willing to admit she knew a lot about it. One hot August afternoon, she wrote, she was in the kitchen preparing dinner for ten. Although the house was full of people, no one offered to help her chop, stir, or set the table. She was stewing in her own juices, she said, when her seventy-eight-year-old mother and her two small children insisted that she stop what she was doing and take them swimming.

They positioned themselves in the car, she said, leaning on the horn and shouting her name out the window so all the neighbors could hear them, loudly reminding her that she had promised to take them to the pond. That, Gordon said, was when she lost it. She flew outside and jumped on the hood of the car. She pounded on the windshield. She told her mother and her children that she was never, ever going to take any of them anywhere and none of them was ever going to have one friend in any house of hers until the hour of their death—which, she said, she hoped was soon.

Then the frightening thing happened. "I became a huge bird," she said. "A carrion crow. My legs became hard stalks, my eyes were sharp and vicious. I developed a murderous beak. Greasy black feathers took the place of arms. I flapped and flapped. I blotted out the sun's light with my flapping." Even after she had been forced off the hood of the car, she said, it took her a while to come back to herself and when she did she was appalled, because she realized she had genuinely frightened her children. Her son said to her, "I was scared because I didn't know who you were."

"Sin makes the sinner unrecognizable," Gordon concluded, and the only antidote to it is forgiveness, but the problem is that anger is so exciting, so enlivening, that forgiveness can seem like a limp surrender. If you have ever cherished a resentment, you know how right it can make you feel to have someone in the world whom you believe is all wrong. You may not be up to admitting it yet, but one of the great benefits of having an enemy is that you get to look good by comparison. It also helps to have someone to blame for why your life is not turning out the way it was supposed to.

Last Friday on National Public Radio I heard Linda Wirtheimer talking to a correspondent in the Middle East about the amazing things that are happening there between Israelis and Palestinians. "How are people reacting?" she asked him. "After all, losing an enemy is as upsetting as losing a friend." I hadn't thought about it that way before, but she is right. When you allow your enemy to stop being your enemy, all the rules change. Nobody knows how to act anymore, because forgiveness is an act of transformation. It does not offer the adrenaline rush of anger, nor the feeling of power that comes from a well-established resentment. It is a quiet revolution, as easy to miss as a fist uncurling to become an open hand, but it changes people in ways that anger only wishes it could.

So why don't we do it more often? Because it is scary, to lay down your arms like that, to trade in your pride and your power on the off-chance that you may discover something more valuable than either of them. "To forgive," writes Mary Gordon, "is to give up the exhilaration of one's own unassailable rightness." And there is loss in that, only it is the loss of an illusion, and what is gained is unmistakably real: the chance to live again, free from the bitterness that draws the sweetness from our lives, that gives us scary faces and turns us into carrion crows who blot out the sun with our flapping. No one else does this to us. We do it to ourselves, but we do not have to.

We are being forgiven every day of our lives. We are being set free by someone who has arranged things so that we have all the advantages. We have choices. We have will. And we have an advocate, who seems to know that we need lots of practice at this forgiveness business. How often should we forgive? Will seven times take care of it? "Not seven times," Jesus said, "but, I tell you, seventy-seven times." This is no chore. This is a promise, because forgiveness is the way of life. It is God's cure for the deformity our resentments cause us. It is how we discover our true shape, and every time we do it we get to be a little more alive. What God knows and we don't yet is that once we get the hang of it, seventy times seven won't be enough, not to mention seventy-seven. We'll be so carried away by it that we'll hope it never ends.

Family Values

Do you think that I have come to bring peace to the earth? No, I tell you, but rather division! (Luke 12:51)

THOSE OF US who listen to television talk shows hear a lot about "family values," especially during an election season. Everyone is worried about them. More and more people blame the breakdown of the family for the growing list of our social problems: for crime and unemployment, for moral lassitude and mental illness. The family is where children learn values, people say. If children do not learn about honesty, hard work, responsibility, and faith from their mothers and fathers, chances are that no one else will be able to teach them those things. When families break down, values break down. And when values break down, families break down. So everyone is all for "family values," although no one can say what that means, exactly.

Jesus, unfortunately, can, and what he says in that regard is a sure sign he could never have gotten himself elected president. "From now on five in one household will be divided," he says, and he goes on to outline the feuds: father and son against each other, mother and daughter against each other, son's wife and son's mother at each other's throats—a whole house full of slamming doors and meals swallowed in stony silence—all because of Jesus.

It is the kind of statement that makes his campaign managers bury their heads in their arms and think about quitting. It is the kind of statement that makes Christians wonder if they are hearing right. Is this really Jesus? Is this the prince of peace who taught us to love our enemies, the gentle shepherd who taught us to turn the other cheek? It is the kind of statement that makes you wish someone had forgotten to write it down, or that someone else had decided to edit it out, but even if we did not have it in Luke we would still have it in Matthew: "Do not think that I have come to bring peace to the earth; I have not come to bring peace, but a sword" (10:34).

What are we to make of such a harsh pronouncement, and where, please, is the good news in it? Let Jesus divide us from our enemies, by all means—from those who hit and hurt and lie and steal, from those who corrupt and destroy the creatures of God—but from our families? From our own parents and our own children, the very people who have taught us what little we know about the love and forgiveness of God?

Now some people never learned those things at home, and they may be in the best position to understand what Jesus is talking about here. They know that blood relation is no guarantee of love or forgiveness, and that sometimes the only way to save your life is to lose your family, closing the door on them and never looking back.

But Jesus is not talking about the ordinary cruelties of family life, as devastating as they can be. He is talking very specifically about the divisions that occur between parents and children, brothers and sisters, husbands and wives, when he walks into their lives. He is talking about what happens to family loyalty when he asks them to put God first in their lives. He is talking about what happens to family harmony when he asks them to choose whom they will follow.

There they are sitting around the dining room table one night, minding their own business, when the gospel falls like a sword across their dining room table and quivers there, with half the roast on one side and half on the other, green beans everywhere. Some of those sitting around the table are struck to the heart. They want to pull the sword out and run straight into the street with it, swinging it above their heads and making perfect strangers listen to what just happened to them.

Others want to clean up the mess and get on with supper. Sure, it is the gospel, but there is no reason to get all upset about it. Being a good Christian is not all that different from being a good citizen, after all. You just stay out of trouble and be nice to your neighbors and say your prayers at night. There is absolutely no reason to go make a spectacle out of yourself.

And then there is always the family member who does not see a thing, who does not believe in swords and who goes right on eating as if nothing ever happened, muttering under his breath about how everyone in this house is stark raving mad.

Do you know other stories like that? Like the parents who raise their children to be doctors and lawyers and have almost succeeded when the last one announces he wants to be a minister, and their faces fall but he goes to seminary anyway, and when they draw up their wills he is not in them? Or like the grown children who find out how much money their elderly parents are giving away to a church-run orphanage in the midwest and who have mom and dad declared mentally incompetent in order to protect their own inheritance? Or like the mother who will not speak to her two adult children because one left the church of his youth for a place where he speaks in tongues and the other refuses to go to church at all?

What is so disturbing about these stories is that Jesus does not say they should not be so. He says, in fact, that they are inevitable, that the gospel is inherently divisive and that we should not be surprised when we fight about it. God's word is "like a hammer that breaks a rock in pieces," says the prophet Jeremiah (23:29), and Jesus does not disagree with him. "Do you think I have come to bring peace on the earth? No, I tell you, but rather division!"

Now on the one hand, you have to remember where Jesus was when he said that. He was on the road to Jerusalem, the city of his certain death, and it was tearing him up inside. "I have a baptism with which to be baptized," he says, "and what stress I am under until it is completed!" He was in a tightening vise, and he had no sympathy for people who tried to squirm out of it themselves, using their family responsibilities as reasons why they could not follow him.

"Let me first go and bury my father," someone asked him. The answer was no. "Let me first say farewell to those at my home," said another, and again the answer was no. Loyalty to God is not one allegiance to be juggled along with all the rest. It is primary. It is not negotiable. It is a matter of life and death, although sometimes you have to be on the road to Jerusalem before you can see it that way.

But Jesus did not become someone else on that road. He did not suddenly change from gentle shepherd to gleaming sword once Jerusalem appeared on the horizon. His ambivalence about his own family was apparent long before that. Way back when he was still a baby, old Simeon took him from his mother's arms and told her what he saw in his eyes. "This child is destined for the falling and the rising of many in Israel," he said to her, "and a sword will pierce your own soul too" (Luke 2:34-35). Then when he was twelve years old and had gone with his parents on pilgrimage to Jerusalem, he deliberately stayed behind when they left for home. After three days of frantic searching, they found him in the temple, sitting among the teachers. "Why have you treated us like this?" they asked him, but he looked at them placidly and said, "Why were you searching for me? Did you not know that I must be in my Father's house?" (Luke 2:49).

But perhaps the most telling encounter came later, when his mother and his brothers came to see him in one of the towns where he was teaching but could not reach him because of all the people. Thinking he would be pleased, someone elbowed a way through the crowd and told Jesus they were there and that they wanted to see him, but he replied: "My mother and my brothers are those who hear the word of God and do it" (Luke 8:21).

That is, I think, very helpful to us. Jesus did not despise the family, but he did redefine it. For him, family was not a matter of whose chromosomes you carry around inside of you but whose image you are created in. It was not a matter of who has the same last name or lives at the same address but who serves the same God, which means that his family became huge beyond counting, with lepers and tax collectors and Roman centurions in it, with scruffy looking men who smelled of fish and ladies in robes made of gold brocade and hordes of squealing children.

There was no family tree in his Holy Bible. As much as his ancestors may have mattered to him, it was more like a family forest he walked around in, with relatives collected from all over the place—some from one family and some from another—all of them gathered in one place because of their allegiance to one father. That was the family where they learned what was right and what was wrong, what was worth living for and what was not. Whatever they had or had not learned at their own parents' knees, that family gave them another chance to discover the love and forgiveness they needed to live. And they squabbled—mercy, how they squabbled, and still do—but with Jesus as their Lord, they remained a family, his family, the one he lived for and the one he was willing to die for, though it ran a sword through his own mother's soul.

Those are his family values, and while they may well send a shiver down our spines, there is good news here for those with the nerve to hear it. The gospel is not a flashlight but a fire. It can warm and it can burn. The gospel is not a table knife but a sword. It can set free and it can divide. The gospel is not pablum. It is powerful stuff, powerful enough to challenge the most sacred human ties, but as frightening as it is, it is not finally to be feared.

The peace of God is worth anything it takes to get there, and anyone knows that the absence of conflict is not peace. The good news is that in Christ God has given us someone worth fighting about, and someone with clout enough to end all our fighting, for his word is like fire, like a hammer that breaks a rock into pieces.

Blessed Brokenness

When he was at the table with them, he took bread, blessed and broke it, and gave it to them. Then their eyes were opened, and they recognized him; and he vanished from their sight. (Luke 24:30-31)

LUKE'S STORY OF what happened on the road to Emmaus is one of seven post-resurrection stories in the gospels, and like all the rest of them it is a little ghostly: the stranger whom the disciples do not recognize at first, who turns out to be the Messiah, who vanishes from their sight as soon as they know who he is. The crucifixion stories are not like this. They are one hundred percent solid. Jesus is nailed to the cross with a nameplate tacked above his head, where he dies in front of a hundred eyewitnesses. No case of mistaken identity here. No sudden appearance and disappearance. His death is real.

His resurrection, on the other hand, is largely rumor. Someone said that someone said his tomb was empty, but that could mean anything. Maybe his body was stolen. Maybe he revived and walked away. It was women who first spread the story, and everyone knew how they embellished things. Even those who saw him in the flesh had a hard time convincing anyone else it was true. Thomas did not buy it, not until he had seen for himself, and seven resurrection stories do not go very far. Jesus did not appear to everyone before he ascended to heaven, which left plenty of people to weigh the evidence for themselves, to listen to the testimony of those who were there and to decide if and what they would believe.

That, in a nutshell, is the situation of the post-Easter church. It was the situation faced by Luke's church, and the churches of the other gospel writers. It was the situation Paul addressed in his letters to the churches of Asia Minor. It is our situation today. None of us was there, for the real death or the rumored resurrection. All of us have a decision to make about the truth of what we have heard. But if it *is* all true, then we have more than hearsay to make up our minds. If the Lord is risen indeed, then we may base our decision on our own encounter with the living God. The question is, what is his address?

For Luke, the answer is: somewhere on the road between here and Emmaus. Luke is the only gospel writer who tells us the story of what happened on that road, but everyone has walked it at one time or another. It is the road you walk when your team has lost, your candidate has been defeated, your loved one has died—the long road back to the empty house, the piles of unopened mail, to life as usual, if life can ever be usual again.

It is the road of deep disappointment, and walking it is the living definition of sad, just like the two disciples in today's story. It takes two hours to walk seven miles, and that is how long they have to talk over the roller coaster events of the past three days. The trial, the crucifixion, the silent procession to the tomb. And then the women's vision of angels, the empty grave. Real death. Rumored resurrection.

They are talking it all over when the stranger comes up behind them and asks them what they are talking about, so that they stop in their tracks to look at him. Who is he, Rip van Winkle? "Are you the only visitor to Jerusalem who does not know the things that have happened there in these days?" Cleopas asks him, but the truth is they are both glad for his company and so they walk with him, matching their stride to his as they tell him everything they know.

They tell him how things had looked so promising at first, when Jesus impressed everyone with his eloquence and mighty acts, and then how things had gone wrong, bad wrong, so that there was finally nothing left for them to do but to go back home, dragging their feet in the dust and dung.

"We had hoped he was the one to redeem Israel," they say to him, admitting their defeat. "We had hoped." Hope in the past tense, one of the saddest sounds a human being can make. We had hoped he was the one. We believed things might really change, but we were wrong. He died. It is over now. No more fairy tales. No more illusions. Back to business as usual.

That is when their walking partner explodes at them. "Oh, how foolish you are, and how slow of heart!" he says to them. Or in other words, "You idiots!" If you had read your Bibles, none of this would come as a surprise to you. It is right there in black and white: the Christ is not the one who wins the power struggle; he is the one who loses it. The Christ is not the undefeated champion; he is the suffering servant, the broken one, who comes into his glory with his wounds still visible. Those hurt places are the proof that he is who he says he is, because the way you recognize the Christ—and his followers—is not by their muscles but by their scars.

Which means that they are not to despise the painful parts of their lives anymore. Which means that they are not to interpret their defeats as failures anymore. Which means that they are not to fear their enemies anymore, not even death itself. Contrary to all good common sense, they are to follow their leader into the scariest, more dangerous places in the world armed with nothing but a first-aid kit, because they, like him, are not fighters but physicians—wounded healers—whose credentials are their own hurt places.

Starting with Moses and working his way through the prophets, the stranger opens the scriptures to them and they hang on his words. He is a gifted preacher, but it is more than that. They are wounded, and what he is telling them is good, good news. Maybe they aren't losers after all. Maybe the rumors are true. Maybe there is reason to resurrect their crucified hope.

So when they arrive at their village and he shakes their hands goodbye, they will not let him go. They have not gotten enough of him yet, so they invite him to stay with them and he does. He is an odd guest, though. It is their house, their food, their table, but when the three of them sit down together, it is he, the guest, who acts as host, who reaches out, takes the bread, says the blessing, breaks the bread, and gives it to them. Maybe it is the oddness of the act that makes the shingles fall from their eyes, or maybe it is the familiarity of it—something they have seen him do before on a green hillside with five loaves and two fish, in an upper room with unleavened bread and passover wine. He takes, blesses, breaks, gives—and through the torn, fragrant edges of the loaf he holds out to them, they look at him and know who he is, one moment before he vanishes from their sight.

Not too long ago I heard two children talking about this story. "How do you know when you are blind?" one of them asked. "You don't," the other one said. "You only know afterward, when you can see."

The blindness of the two disciples does not keep their Christ from coming to them. He does not limit his post-resurrection appearances to those with full confidence in him. He comes to the disappointed, the doubtful, the disconsolate. He comes to those who do not know their Bibles, who do not recognize him even when they are walking right beside him. He comes to those who have given up and are headed back home, which makes this whole story a story about the blessedness of brokenness.

Maybe that is only good news if you happen to be broken. If you are not, then I guess it would be better news to hear a story about how those who believe in God may skip right over the broken part and go straight to the wholeness part, but that does not seem to be the case. Jesus seems to prefer working with broken people, with broken dreams, in a broken world. If someone hands him a whole loaf, he will take it, bless it, break it, and give it, and he will do the same thing with his own flesh and blood, because that is the way of life God has shown him to show the rest of us: to take what we have been given, whether we like it or not, and to bless it—to say thank you for it—whether it is the sweet, satisfying bread of success or the tear-soaked bread of sorrow. To say thank you and to break it because that is the only way it can be shared, and to hand it around, not to eat it all by ourselves but to find someone to eat it with, so that the broken loaf may bring all of us broken ones together into one body, where we may recognize the risen Lord in our midst.

Beginning to end, Luke's story of what happened on the road to Emmaus is a perfect little address book for the living God. First there is the closeness of the two disciples on the road, and then their kindness to a stranger. Then there is the way their hearts burned within them when he opened the scriptures to them, and how they knew him in the breaking of the bread. Count them—fellowship, hospitality, word, and sacrament—all the ways Christ has promised to be present with us, which also happen to be the everyday activities of the church. Not the building, or the institution, but the people of God—us—who attend to one another, to strangers, to God's word and sacraments as a way of life.

A lot of it happens other places, but the breaking of bread at holy communion can break you right open. Sometimes you can be right in the middle of it when suddenly the tears start rolling down. It is like the gates to your heart have opened and everything you have ever loved comes tumbling out to be missed and praised and mourned and loved some more. It is like being known all the way down. It is like being in the presence of God. One moment you see him and the next you do not. One moment your eyes are opened and you recognize the risen Christ, and the next he vanishes from your sight.

Take heart. This is no ghost. Do not fear. You cannot lose him for good. This is the place he has promised to be, and this is the place he returns to meet us again and again. Risen Lord, be known to us in the breaking of the bread.

Promises

Refreshing
God's Memory

This is the sign of the covenant that I make between me and you and every living creature that is with you, for all future generations: I have set my bow in the clouds, and it shall be a sign of the covenant between me and the earth. (Genesis 9:12-13)

I DO NOT KNOW anyone whose spirits are not improved by a rainbow. It does not seem to matter where you are—stuck in rush hour traffic on a Friday afternoon or sitting on a screened porch watching the wind blow foam across the lake. The point is that you are not expecting anything. It is raining, and your soul has fallen silent under the drumming on the roof. All plans are cancelled. There is nothing to do but wait it out and so you sit there, sniffing all the things you cannot smell when they are dry—the street, the grass, the earth, the dog. The wet air is heavy in your nose. It lies against your face like a washcloth while you wait for the clouds to pass.

It is easy to lose track of time when it is raining, since rain has a way of triggering memory. Before you know it, you are five years old again, sliding down a muddy bank in back of your house while the rain beats your hair flat against your head. The taste of it in your mouth is sweet and salt—part sky, part you. It runs into your eyes, your ears. It runs down the back of your neck, cold, the best bath you ever had. The sky is gray as a dolphin, or was, last time you looked. Now you look up and there it is—a perfect arch of purest color—a rainbow, where you least expected it.

27

What a wonderful idea! Who in the world thought of that? I know people who are otherwise unsuperstitious who still get quiet when they see a rainbow. They know it is just a trick the sun plays—the refraction of light in drops of water—but it sure does look like an omen, or a blessing.

In his novel *Angle of Repose*, Wallace Stegner tells the story of Oliver and Susan Ward, who raised a family on the western frontier late in the last century. While Susan labors with her fourth child after having lost her third, Oliver stands outside their cabin and watches the sun go down with his eldest son Ollie. Pacing back and forth in front of the shack, Oliver disappears from view, down to the corner of the cabin where Ollie hears him mutter, "Good Lord, look at that." Ollie hurries down to where his father is standing and sees him staring into the evening sky, where two rainbows perch one on top of the other, bright as colored glass, stretching from horizon to horizon. Oliver goes quickly to Susan's door, tapping at it with his fingernails. "Sue?" he says, "Sue, if you're able, look outside. There's an absolute sign, the most perfect double rainbow you ever saw." The door opens and the doctor stands in it. "Your wife isn't interested in rainbows," he says to Oliver. "You've got a daughter three minutes old."

A friend of mine remembers his own rainbow omen. When he was an eight-year-old boy in Macon, Georgia, he was inside listening to the radio when he heard the news that World War II was over. Running into the street, he found his entire neighborhood there, all of them cheering and crying and falling into each other's arms. He does not remember who saw it first, but someone said, "Look!" and pointed down the street, where the oak trees parted to reveal the top of a bright rainbow. All at once the street got quiet as a prayer. "It was God's promise of peace," he says now, "and we all knew it."

The story of God, Noah, and the rainbow is one of the stories that has gotten down deep inside of us, so deep that most of us make the connection my friend made without even thinking about it. The rainbow is God's promise of peace—God's everlasting covenant with all creation—and it is hard to see one without experiencing a measure of that peace. The rainbow is God's pure gift to us, a colorful corrective for anyone who believes that all the grace in the Bible is in the New Testament. It is not. The sacred story is full of grace from the very beginning, although we have always had a perverse way of fighting it off. It is almost as if we cannot stand too much good news.

God says, "I choose you to be my partners. Will you choose me?" and we say sure, but before you know it we have got our sticky fingers in the till, embezzlers from the word go. That is what happened in today's story, anyway. God made the whole world in one whirlwind week, pronounced it all good, yes, very good, and gave us the keys to the whole creation, with one notable exception. A fruit tree—one fruit tree, with a picket fence around it and a small sign that said, "Private stock. Please do not pick."

Last week I visited a friend of mine who is a folk artist and she showed me her version of what happened with the fruit tree. In her picture, a beautiful brown woman reaches up to pluck a piece of fruit while a gorilla holds his hands up like a policeman stopping traffic and a leopard sharpens her claws on the trunk of the tree. Meanwhile, the fruit on the forbidden tree looks suspiciously like South Carolina peaches.

"What are those?" I asked, pointing at the rosy-gold fruit. "Well," she said, "the Bible doesn't say what kind of fruit it was, and I figured no one was going to be tempted by an apple if they could have a peach instead." And you know she was right. Someone *was* tempted, and before the new creation had even dried off, there it was broken—first the trespass with the fruit, then the hiding from God in the garden, then the shameful, sad eviction, which even God could not stand. Before sending them out of Eden forever, God made Adam and Eve their first set of clothes. Can you picture that? The Lord God Almighty, bent over some stiff animal skins with a needle and thread, so the poor pale creatures would have something to pull around them when they walked out the gates for the last time. Grace, from the very beginning.

But things got worse, not better. Adam and Eve's son Cain killed his brother Abel—the first murder but not the last—and humankind went on breaking what God had made until, by the sixth chapter of Genesis, God ran out of pity. "I will blot out from the earth the human beings I have created," God said, "people together with animals and creeping things and birds of the air, for I am sorry that I have made them" (6:7). That may be the most sobering sentence in the whole Bible. What a fast catastrophe, to go from "God saw everything that he had made, and indeed, it was very good" to "I am sorry that I have made them," in five short chapters.

There was one person who found favor in the sight of the Lord, however, and to him God gave the blueprint for an ark. All of us who have heard the story have imagined it: the big, roofed boat, looking more like a floating barn than a boat, filled to the rafters with life—zebras, flamingos, king snakes, box turtles, barn owls, giraffes, hyenas, ground-hogs—all of them floating above the wet chaos below, where the rest of creation was perishing, seeking higher and higher ground until there was none left, and then surrendering their last bubbles of air as the waters closed over their heads.

It was awful, make no mistake about it. We focus on Noah and his zoo because they survived, but no one and nothing else did. The cleansing was complete. The destruction was total, and when the waters subsided it was like Hurricane Andrew had circled the entire globe. God had willed it, but the result was so devastating that God willed never to will such a thing again. "I establish my covenant with you," God said to Noah when it was all over, "that never again shall all flesh be cut off by the waters of a flood, and never again shall there be a flood to destroy the earth" (Genesis 9:11). As a sign of the covenant, God set a rainbow in the clouds—not to jog Noah's memory but to jog God's own. "When the bow is in the clouds, I will see it and remember," God said, and the creation was back on dry ground again.

The history of the world, biblically speaking, is the history of God's promises to humankind. When we tell the sacred story, we tend to organize our telling around these promises—the promise of peace to Noah, the promise of a land and a nation to Abraham and Sarah, the promise of the law to Moses, the promise of a son to Mary. They are all the same promise, at heart—the promise of intimate relationship with God—but that one promise has taken different forms over the years, as God has struggled to remain faithful to the orneriest bunch of partners a deity ever had.

"Covenant" is the Bible's word for this strange and strong relationship. Established by God in creation, the covenant has survived floods and famines, wars and tumults, the rising and falling of empires. The prosperity of our own culture may be the worst blow the covenant has ever been dealt, but it has survived that too, and to this day, the promise holds. "I shall be your God and you shall be my people." That is the heart of it—our belonging to God, God's belonging to us—the covenant of intimate relationship with God.

Many of us hear an "if" at the end of it. "I shall be your God and you shall be my people—*if* you obey my laws, *if* you heed my commandments, *if* you sell all that you own and follow me." We are right to expect something like that, since most covenants are very clear about what each partner will and will not do, but God's covenant with Noah has no conditions in it whatsoever. There is not one word in it about what Noah will and will not do. It is all about what God will and will not do. "I won't hurt you like this again," God promises Noah. "I won't hurt the earth like this again. I won't do it and I won't forget, because I'm hanging up my bow where I can see it—not a weapon anymore, but a reminder of the covenant between me and you and every living creature that is with you, for all future generations."

That is what God said to the whole water-logged bunch of them—not just to Noah and his family, but to all the

31

thin, bewildered animals who were standing around the ramp of the ark with them. The musk ox whose hide had begun to mildew, and the horse who had foundered from standing in water, and the hawk who had all but forgotten how to fly—they were all included in the covenant God made that day. The birds, the animals, the creeping things—every living creature that came out of the ark. "I will not hurt you like this again," God said to all of them that day. "From now on I am in the protection business, not the destruction business. From this day forth, you are all my partners, and your lives are as precious to me as my own."

What in the world has happened? you may well ask. At the beginning of the story, God was mad enough to drown the whole earth. But here at the end something major has shifted in the divine mind. Humankind will not change. The God who knows everything knows that. In no time at all, Jacob will be stealing Esau's birthright, Aaron will be dancing around a golden calf, and David will be figuring out how to get Bathsheba's husband out of town. So the story of the flood is not a story about a change in humankind. It is a story about a change in God, who swears off retribution as a way of dealing with creation and chooses relationship instead.

From now on, God will not repay betrayal with betrayal. From now on, God will not let his sorrow lead him to kill. He will bind himself to his creation in peace, promising himself to it although he knows how it will wound him. So God will be wounded. So be it. With this first, remarkable covenant, God chooses to ally himself with his cantankerous creation whatever the cost. If there is to be pain in the world, then God will share it. Never again will he protect himself from it by killing off those who have caused it. God's promise to them is life, not death, "an everlasting covenant between God and every living creature of all flesh that is on the earth."

Of course bad things continue to happen to us, but this covenant is our assurance that none of them is rooted in God's ill will toward us. God is our ally, not our enemy.

God's will for us is life, not death, and that includes life for every living creature—not just us two-legged ones but also the four-legged ones and the winged ones and those with no legs or wings at all. God's covenant includes clams and trout and snails and snakes. God's covenant includes lizards and centipedes and tadpoles and fireflies. It includes all the species disappearing daily off the face of the earth. They are all of them our covenant partners—heirs of God's promise just like we are—and those of us who understand our kinship with them tremble to think what we have done, killing off those to whom God has promised life.

Just because there are no conditions in Noah's covenant does not make us merely recipients of it. We are creatures made in the image of our creator, after all, which makes us partners in God's plan. We too are allies of creation. We too are lovers of life, which means that we too are wounded by the brokenness we see around us, the brokenness in which we ourselves participate. We are both the breakers and the healers, set into relationship with a God whose covenant calls us to shift the balance from death to life whenever and wherever we can. ·

It is still raining, you see. The story is not over yet, but those of us who have heard it before have a distinct advantage over those who have not, because we know something about how it turns out in the end. In our own time, the ark does not look so much like a barn floating on a choppy sea. It looks more like a blue-green ball bobbing on the dark ocean of space. Inside its gauzy atmosphere, there are black rhinos prowling the thorn bushes of the Serengetti and garlands of monarch butterflies hanging from eucalyptus trees in California; there are baby chimney sweeps cheeping in suburban fireplaces and coyotes howling in desert canyons. There are children in the Sudan eating hibiscus blossoms because there is nothing else left for them to eat and there are war-wrecked men and women who never leave their post at the small window of the ark, wondering when, please God when, will the dove return with the olive leaf in her beak.

We have all of us got a place in that ark—not because we, like Noah and his crew, are all that righteous, but because it has pleased God to preserve our lives. Because life is sacred to God, and having destroyed it once, God has promised never to do it again. If we go on perishing, it may have less to do with divine fiat than with our own amnesia. We have forgotten who we are and what we are supposed to be doing. We have forgotten whose covenant partners we are and how that covenant—not to mention that God—means for us to be bailing water and handing out life vests as fast as we can, so that every living creature who rides this ark with us may share the unmitigated joy of walking down the rickety ramp to plant a foot, a paw, a hoof on dry land.

So God is not the only one who needs a rainbow. We need one too, a reminder of the covenant between God and all creation, between us and every creature who shares the breath of life with us. However stuffy the air may get inside the ark, we can still, like God, remember. We can search the sky for the sign we know is there, even when we cannot see it. We can stay awake to it, and to God, and to one another, until the next time we look up and see it—a perfect curve of color, stretching clear across the sky: God's everlasting Yes to all who live in its embrace.

The Late Bloomer

As for me, this is my covenant with you: You shall be the ances-
tor of a multitude of nations. No longer shall your name be
Abram, but your name shall be Abraham; for I have made you
the ancestor of a multitude of nations. (Genesis 17:4-5)

WHEN THE LORD showed up at Abram's ninety-ninth birthday party, it was not the first time the two had met. That
had happened two dozen years before, when Abram was a
mere youth of seventy-five. "Go from your country and your
kindred and your father's house to the land that I will show
you," God had said to him then, and Abram had gone, taking everything he owned except a map, because there wasn't
one. God's voice was the only map he had, and he and his
wife Sarai learned to live by it, though it led them down to
Egypt and back again. They simply learned to recognize the
tug inside of them when it came, as if God held the end of a
delicate thread stitched lightly through their hearts, and
they learned to follow its lead without having to know
where or what or why.

They just went, that was all, moving so often that they
got their belongings down to a tent full of the bare necessi-
ties. It was just the two of them, after all. Once upon a time
they had planned to have children, but as each year turned
into the next they learned that having a plan was not
enough. Something more was required, something they apparently did not have, and eventually they got used to their
quiet evenings alone. It was just as well. Abram was worn
out by the end of the day, and while he tried to read, Sarai
found him asleep in his chair more often than not. She,
meanwhile, was getting stiff in the knees, so that bending

down to reach a spoon she had dropped became a lengthy ordeal of cranking herself down and up again like one of the camels that dozed in the moonlight outside. What did she think she would do with a toddler?

They would have given up, but the Lord would not let them. Every time they got used to their lives and decided that things were fine just the way they were, the Lord would show up and repeat the promise. "To your offspring I will give this land," God said. "Raise your eyes now, and look from the place where you are, northward and southward and eastward and westward; for all the land that you see I will give to you and to your offspring forever" (Genesis 12:7; 13:14-15). Finally Abram had had enough. "What offspring?" he asked, well into his eighties. "You have given me no children, and my servant Eliezer stands to inherit everything I own."

"But he won't," God said. "Your own son shall be your heir." Then God brought Abram outside and told him to look up, where an eternity of stars pulsed, caught in the vast net of the night sky. "Count them if you can," God said, "and imagine every one of them calling you 'Great Grandfather,' for so shall your descendants be." And Abram believed the Lord. It was too good to be true. It was too ridiculous to be true, but that was the night Abram gave up deciding why it could or could not be true. He simply believed what he had been told and settled down to wait for it.

Sarai, meanwhile, had not been in on the midnight summit and she grew tired of waiting. When her arthritis got so bad she could no longer even rub the knots out of Abram's shoulders, she sent him in to her Egyptian maid Hagar. "It's time we had some children around this place," she said, "even if I can't have them. Why don't you and Hagar get to know each other better?" And they did, but surrogate parenting didn't work much better then than it does now. Hagar got pregnant, and Sarai got hurt, and it was only through the direct intervention of the Lord that Abram's son Ishmael was born and raised in his father's house.

As far as Abram and Sarai knew, that was it: Ishmael was the child God had promised them and while it was not exactly the arrangement they had in mind, they accepted it out of deference to God's wishes. When Ishmael learned to talk, he learned to call two women "Mother," and when he got old enough to walk, Abram took him on long hikes through the countryside, showing him the far horizons of what would one day be his. Sometimes, when Abram looked at the boy, he thought he could see a bit of Sarai's fire in his eye, a little hint of her proud spirit in the way he held his head, and that made Abram feel better about the whole thing. So what if the boy was half Egyptian? Abram could raise him as an Israelite and teach him to love Israel's God.

That is how they lived for thirteen years, until Ishmael's face broke out and his voice began to change and his father Abram prepared for his ninety-ninth birthday. It had been decades since the Lord first appeared to Abram and promised him a land, and at least a decade since the Lord came back to promise him a son. Abram was content on both counts, an old man who had made peace with his life and with his God. All the same, there were still nights Sarai found him outside in the dark, staring up at the sky. When she would walk up beside him she could see the stars shining in his rheumy eyes. "What are you doing?" she would ask him quietly. "Nothing," he would answer her, and then she would take his hand and he would let her lead him back inside.

Then, when Abram was one year short of a hundred years old, the Lord appeared to him again, renewing the covenant between them. "I am God Almighty," God said, by way of self-identification, only God did not speak English to Abram. "I am El Shaddai," God said in Hebrew, and it was a very big birthday present, for God to give Abram the divine name like that. A good Hebrew would never presume to speak nor even to know the name of God, and while this name was an earlier name than the name God gave to Moses, it was a name all the same, which was God's way of inviting Abram into closer relationship.

"I am El Shaddai," God said. "Walk before me, and be blameless. And I will make my covenant between me and you, and will make you exceedingly numerous" (Genesis 17:1-2). This was not news to Abram. He had heard it before, but one thing to know about a covenant is that it is a living thing, as surely as if it had a beating heart and blood flowing in its veins. Its life thrives on its revival, and every time it is uttered the promise is renewed. Every time God appeared to Abram and said it all again, it was like the sky had sprung a rainbow. God remembered. Abram and Sarai remembered. The covenant was renewed.

On this particular occasion, God decided to give the old couple a daily reminder of what lay in store for them. He changed Abram's name to Abraham, meaning "father of a multitude of nations," and Sarai's name he changed to Sarah, for "kings of peoples shall come from her." There was a lot of laughter all around about that. First Abraham fell down laughing, and a little later Sarah had a big guffaw of her own—only God was serious. The royal family tree of Israel would begin with these two strong brown roots, and henceforth they would remember that every time anyone called them by their new names: Father of a Multitude and his wife Queen.

There was a minor string attached, of course—not a condition of the covenant but a sign of it—to go along with the new names. "Every male among you shall be circumcised," God said, and I am glad I was not there when Abraham found out what that meant. "You want us to do *what?*" But promises call forth other promises—not as a way of earning the covenant but as a way of affirming it—and it made sense that a promise concerning Abraham's descendants should call forth a promise about the part of him that would plant the seeds of those descendants. Ouch.

"Okay, I will do this as a sign of our relationship," Abraham said, and circumcision became the sign of God's chosen people, who surrendered to El Shaddai the very means of their survival. Abraham limped around the house for a couple of days after that, but the pain—like the name—was a constant reminder of the Almighty God who had chosen him and Sarah as partners.

Abraham's household had grown quite a bit by that time. There were not only Sarah, Hagar, and Ishmael, but a whole host of servants and their families who lived with them, and I expect there was a good bit of confusion until everyone got used to the new names. If you have ever been close to someone who decided to go from being "Bobby" to being "Robert" or from being Ms. Sharon Smith to being Mrs. Sharon Thistlethwaite, then you know how many times you can get it wrong before you finally get it right.

Names are very important, and when someone's name changes, something inside that person usually changes along with it—or wants to change along with it—but it can be hard to get other people to go along, since most of us do not like change. We like things to stay the same. They're easier that way, and meanwhile we can pretend that the world is a safe and stable place where we will always know who is who and what is what. Fortunately, "Abraham and Sarah" was pretty close to "Abram and Sarai," but that turned out not to be the problem. The problem was what the names meant.

Every time someone forgot and called him Abram, Abraham would say, "It's Abraham now, remember?" and the person in question would say, "Right. Father of a Multitude. How could I forget?" That is what he would say to Abraham's face, but as he walked away you could hear him muttering under his breath, "Father of a multitude! Who does he think he's kidding? He is the father of one pimply adolescent, and the minute the old man dies, the boy's mother will be down at the bus station buying two tickets back to Egypt. Father of a multitude! Give me a break."

It was even worse for Sarah. Hagar simply stopped addressing her by name at all. She called her "ma'am," or "mistress." Whenever she could, she found someone else to carry messages to Sarah for her—anything to avoid calling her rival by the name "Queen." Why hadn't God changed *her* name? That is what Hagar wanted to know. *She* was the one who had borne Abraham a son, not Sarah, but her name was still "Hagar, Sarah's maid," and it galled her to no end. Ishmael, on the other hand, was quick to use Sarah's new name, only she could not stop thinking she heard a taunt in his voice when he said it. Nothing blatant enough for Abraham to catch and scold him for—just enough to bring a hot blush to her cheeks and make her wish that Ishmael would go outside to play.

The one voice she would have thought safe was Abraham's voice, but even it wounded her. "Good night, Sarah," he said, and she could hear the hope in it—that the promise would come true soon, that any day now she would come to him drying her hands on her dress and say, "Abraham, I have something to tell you." Only she did not have anything to tell him, not yet, and every barren day that went by made her new name weigh heavier on her heart. "Sarah, mother of nations." Okay, she would wear that name like the hairshirt it was, but how long would she have to suffer it? How many more years before the long fast was over and the feasting began?

It is hard thing, to believe in a promise—to live by it, day after day, to see it in the night sky and hear it in your name and see it again in your lover's eyes. It is a hard thing, to believe in a promise with no power to make it come true. Everything is in the future tense—the land, the son, the blessing. Everything *will* happen, by and by, but in the meantime what is there to live on *now*?

And yet. What better way to live than in the grip of a promise, and a divine one at that? Who in her right mind would give that back? To wake every morning to the possibility that today might be the day. To remain wide awake all day long, noticing everything—the way the shade of the olive tree processes from west to east, and how the smell of the fields changes from green grass to yellow hay as the sun heats up overhead. To search the face of every stranger in case it turns out to be an angel of God. To take nothing for granted. Or to take everything as granted, though not yet grasped. To handle every moment of one's life as a seed of the promise and to plant it tenderly, never knowing if this moment, or the next, may be the one that grows.

To live like that is to discover that the blessing is not future but now. The promise may not be fully in hand. It may still be on the way, but to live reverently, deliberately, and fully awake—that is what it means to live in the promise, where the wait itself is as rich as its end. All it takes are some regular reminders, because as long as the promise is renewed, the promise is alive, as vivid as a rainbow, as real as the million stars overhead.

That is what Abraham and Sarah found out, anyway. For two dozen years they lived in the promise, led by the delicate threads stitched through their hearts. For two dozen years they watered every seed that fell upon their paths without losing sight of where they were going or who had set them on their way. There were lean times and there were fat ones, but insofar as they were all God's times, they were all good times, rolling out ahead of the old couple like a red carpet for them to walk upon. Never did this seem more true to either of them than the spring morning of Sarah's ninetieth year, when she came in to her husband drying her hands on her dress and said (with stars for eyes), "Abraham, I have something to tell you."

Peculiar Treasures

Now therefore, if you obey my voice and keep my covenant, you shall be my treasured possession out of all the peoples. Indeed, the whole earth is mine, but you shall be for me a priestly kingdom and a holy nation. (Exodus 19:5-6)

MOST OF YOU, I am sure, saw the movie *The Ten Commandments* long before I did. I did not get around to it until a couple of years ago, when a movie theater in Atlanta announced a revival of Cecil B. DeMille's masterpiece. When I called for show times I found there were only two a day—it was a long movie—but I was determined to see it, so I packed a turkey sandwich, a thermos of sweet tea, and entered the theater for the better part of a Saturday afternoon. Once the lights went down and the film began, I lost all track of time. It was not just a movie. It was an experience, spectacular at some times and silly at others, but what struck me hardest was the conviction behind it all. When that movie was made, it was not offered for entertainment alone. There was a higher purpose at work in it, something the filmmaker and his 1950s audience agreed upon: that this story was seminal to their life as a people and a nation, and that their ongoing obedience to God's law was crucial to the continuation of that life.

These days I am not so sure. When Charlton Heston came down from Mount Sinai carrying a stone tablet of the law propped on each forearm, even I laughed, because his hair was all fluffed up, like his encounter with the Almighty had electrified it and he had not gotten it back under control again. But maybe that was the best Cecil B. DeMille could do. He had to do *something*, after all, to show the change that had taken place.

When Moses went up the mountain, he was Moses the liberator of the people—those long-time heirs of God's promise whose inheritance was finally coming due. God's covenant with their grandfather Abraham had three shining jewels in it: descendants as plentiful as the stars in the sky, a special relationship to God, and a land of milk and honey all their own. The people themselves were living proof that the first part of the promise had come true. They lived by the grace of the second and they were on their way to the third, but something was still missing, something Moses went up the mountain to get.

When he went up the mountain, he was Moses the liberator, but when he came back down again, fairly scorched by his encounter with the Lord, he was Moses the lawgiver, bearing on his arms the two tablets of the law that God had given him for the people. They were short; they were to the point. There were ten of them, one for each finger, so that even a child could remember them—four "Thou shalt's" and six "Thou shalt not's"—covering every aspect of the people's relationship with God and one another. They contained no fine print. If the people had been at all confused about the shape of their life with God, their questions were answered. The covenant was right there, blasted in stone, for anyone to see.

But what a change! For centuries, their relationship with God had been all grace, no law. God had made promises to Noah and to Abraham without asking anything in return. In both cases, it was God who was bound by the covenant and humankind who was set free. "I shall establish my covenant with you," God promised Noah, "that never again shall all flesh be cut off by the waters of a flood." "I shall make of you a great nation," God promised Abraham, "and I shall give to you, and to your descendants after you, the land of your sojournings." But now, suddenly, the divine "I shall's" have stopped. The tables have turned and the "Thou shalt's" have begun. The covenant with Moses involves ob-

43

ligations. Chosen people are expected to behave in chosen ways, and for the first time in the history of the world, formal religious law comes into the picture.

Why now? According to the tenth chapter of Exodus, *now* because the promise has begun to come true. Just three months earlier, God had stymied the Egyptians and borne Israel forth on eagle's wings. "You have seen what I did," God says to Moses. "Now, therefore, if you will obey my voice and keep my covenant, you shall be my own possession among all peoples." That is how the "Thou shalt's" begin. "Because I have done what I said I would do, now it is your turn to show what you can do." That is a modern translation of what God says to Moses. "Because I have, now, therefore, thou shalt."

Only there is no coercion here, no strong-arm God forcing people to do things. "*If* you will obey my voice," God says. "I am about to spell it all out for you, so that there is no question about how a holy nation acts, but I cannot choose it for you. Only you can do that. If you do, however, you shall be my own possession among all peoples."

Those of you who use the King James Version of the Bible are used to a different translation here. "Ye shall be a peculiar treasure unto me above all people," God says in Elizabethan English, and it is one of the sweetest phrases in all of Hebrew scripture. The original word is *segulla*—a king's treasure—some of it acquired by conquest and some of it given in friendship, all of it together the sign of the king's sovereignty, the adornment of the royal throne. "Ye shall be a peculiar treasure unto me," God says to the people, "if you will obey my voice and keep my covenant."

There is no doubt about it. This is conditional language, and those who know their Bibles have heard it before. "You are my friends, if you do what I command you," Jesus says in the fifteenth chapter of John. On the one hand, it makes sense. In order to be the Lord's friends, in order to be God's peculiar treasure, there are certain things we must do. God will grant us special relationship as a reward for our obedience. That makes sense.

44

But on the other hand, what a crashing disappointment that God's love should be offered to us the same way so much human love is, with conditions on our behavior. For most of us, it started before we could talk. Mom was all smiles until the third glass of milk sailed off the high chair and exploded against the wall. Dad thought playing darts was fun until one missed the target and landed quivering in his foot. It was the same way at school. Correct answers made the teacher's eyes glow, but snicker once behind her back and a sudden chill fell over the room.

Even the playground was not safe. The score was four to three when you came to bat—two outs, bases loaded. Even your teammates groaned when you stepped onto the plate. Softball was not your game, but it was not as if you had a choice. It was your turn. Everyone had to take a turn. So you swung and you swung and you swung, each time hoping for a miracle—for the crack of leather hitting wood, for the shock of it traveling up your skinny arms—but no. "You're out!" someone cried, and the game was over, and no one talked to you in the lunchroom that day.

Over and over, it is the same lesson: perform well and we will love you. Foul up and you are on your own. It is not that blatant, of course. It is not even that conscious, but still it is often how we act. If you do what I want you to do, I will spend more time with you. If you behave the way I want you to behave, I will tell you what a good person you are. Conditional love. I will love you "if...." The fear that gets cranked up inside of us by language like that is not the fear of being thought bad people, however. It is the fear of being abandoned. It is the fear of being left all alone. That is why it is so hard to hear God say, "if...."

"Now, therefore, if you will obey my voice and keep my covenant, you shall be my own possession among all peoples." And if we do not? What happens to us if we fail? Will God dump the treasure out on the ground for passers-by to fight over, or just melt it down and start over again? Is there any love loose in the world for people like us, who spill our milk and miss the ball and who still have this fierce hunger, this crying need, for someone to look right at the mess we have made and say, "It is all right. I still love you. I will always love you, no matter what"?

At Mount Sinai, God gave the chosen people two very valuable gifts—the law and a renewal of the promise—and ever since then we have been trying to figure out how the two fit together. Do we have to obey the law in order to earn the promise? That is how it sounds, but it does not really work that way. Moses himself was a murderer. Who was he to carry a tablet that said, "Thou shalt not kill"?

And what about the rest of that rowdy crowd? By the time Moses finally came down from the mountain with the law balanced on his arms, everyone down below had given up on him. When he walked into camp, the first thing he saw was his own brother Aaron putting the ears on a little golden calf while all the people danced around it, and Moses let the tablets crash to the ground. He let them break, but only because the people had already broken them. When they came over to see what had happened, all they saw were some broken pieces of stone on the ground. "You shall have no other," they read on one of them, and then they saw the rest: "gods before me."

If the relationship had been based on obeying the law, then that would have been it right there—ten commandments, wrecked before they were ever delivered. But that was not it. Moses pleaded with God on behalf of the people. "Remember Abraham, Isaac, and Israel, your servants," Moses begged. "Remember what you said to them? 'I will multiply your descendants like the stars of heaven, and all this land that I have promised I will give to your descendants, and they shall inherit it forever'" (Exodus 32:13). Moses reminded God of the promise, in other words, and the Lord repented of the evil which he had thought to do to the people.

So that makes it sound like the promise voids the law, only that really does not work either, because promise without law is like a tent without tent poles. It is amorphous. It will not hold up. It looks one way to one person and another way to the next, with no way to tell which way is right. The promise, meanwhile, has a very particular shape to it, and being heirs of it does not mean that anything goes. God knows there are ways of life that work and ways of life that do not work, and the whole point of the promise is to give people a way of life that works.

Which brings us back to the covenant with Moses. "Here," God said, setting ten commandments into stone. "Here are ten rules for a way of life that works.

"*One*. You shall have no other gods before me. In the first place because I am very jealous of your affections and in the second place because other gods cannot do anything for you. I am the one who brought you out of Egypt. I am the Lord your God, and you shall not give anyone else my place in your hearts.

"*Two*. No more golden calves. You look silly bowing down to little statues that you yourselves have made, and besides, you don't need them. You have me.

"*Three*. Don't throw my name around. A name is a very personal thing, and the fact that you know mine at all is a sign of our closeness. Do not abuse the privilege.

"*Four*. Keep the sabbath, not for my sake but for yours. One day a week, stop working and remember that you are more than what you do.

"*Five*. Honor your father and mother. Whatever kind of job they did on you, they are still your roots. Lose them and you lose your place in the story.

"*Six*. Don't murder. However dubious it may seem to you, all life is precious to me, including yours. Until you can make it, don't take it.

"*Seven*. Don't mess around with marriage vows, your own or anyone else's. Sticking with one person is the best chance you have got of growing up.

"*Eight*. Don't take what doesn't belong to you. Life may not be fair, but that doesn't mean you can't be.

"*Nine*. Don't give your word on things you know aren't true. Your word is as much a part of you as your arm or your leg. Twist it and you will limp. Why would you do that to yourself?

"*Ten.* Don't fondle other people's things in your mind as if they were your own. You'll not only resent them for having things; you'll soon resent yourself for not having them too. Learn to want what you have and pretty soon you will have what you want."

These are the ten rules of the covenant with Moses, ten commandments that describe a life worth living. All of them are limits of one kind or another—the lovingly drawn boundaries of a creator bent on reminding creatures of their size—but it is entirely possible to hear them not as conditions on the promise but as part of the promise itself.

"Here is a way of life that works," God says. "Sink these ten posts in the center of your camp, hang a tent on them, and together you may survive the wilderness. Ignore them and you flirt with your own destruction. Guard your life together. Guard your life with me. Here are ten rules that will help you do that. Please accept them as a gift from me."

I am, of course, putting words in God's mouth, which is never a very smart thing to do, but one way or another we are always doing that—sifting through the evidence at hand and then ascribing motives to God that, for all we know, may bend God right in two with laughter. My own motive is to believe in one God, who is both the God of the promise and the God of the law, whose divine will for my obedience does not preclude the divine wish for my love.

I do not, in other words, believe that the Old Testament God is a God of harsh judgment who suddenly melts into a God of pure grace on page one of Matthew's gospel. The grace has been there all along, ever since God could not bear to banish Adam and Eve from the garden of Eden with nothing to wear and made them clothes for their journey away from him.

The covenant with Moses is no sudden imposition of conditions on God's love. It is a natural extension of that love—the careful description of a way of life that will protect the people, so that they may live to enjoy the promise.

Obedience to the law does not earn them the promise. The promise has already been granted to them, unconditionally and forever. Obedience to the law is the sign that they believe the promise. It is how they give witness to their faith, and what they soon find out—for better and for worse—is that there is no reward for keeping the commandments. The wicked still prosper and the good die young, but that does not change a thing. Keeping the commandments is its own reward. Keeping covenant with God is the way of life.

"Now, therefore, if you will obey my voice and keep my covenant, you shall be my peculiar treasure among all peoples." We are truly both. Not only peculiar but also treasure; not only treasure but also peculiar—God's own possession from the beginning of time, the rowdiest bunch of people any God ever tried to love. But love us God does, less because of who we are than because of who God is. The Lord is our God, who brings us out of bondage and bears us on eagle's wings, who gives us the law to preserve our lives, and who, though we earn God's wrath and break God's heart, keeps covenant with us, saying, "It's all right. I still love you. I will always love you, no matter what."

Betrothed by God

I will make for you a covenant on that day with the wild ani-
mals, the birds of the air, and the creeping things of the ground;
and I will abolish the bow, the sword, and war from the land;
and I will make you lie down in safety. (Hosea 2:18)

WHEN THE PROPHET Hosea took Gomer for his wife, it was
a mismatch, to say the least. He was an upright man, a re-
spectable bachelor who could have chosen freely from the
fair maidens of the northern kingdom, but that is not who
God picked out for him. "Go, take a wife of harlotry," God
said to Hosea, "and have children of harlotry, for the land
commits great harlotry by forsaking the Lord." So Hosea,
being a faithful man, did as he was told. He went down to
the local brothel and asked to meet some of the women who
worked there, sitting on the red crushed velvet sofa with his
hands between his knees while he waited for them to come
down. The madam was glad to oblige him, thinking she was
about to get herself a new customer, but when Hosea pro-
posed to Gomer right there in the perfumed parlor and
Gomer said yes, the madam threw them both out into the
street—the sober-looking fellow in the dark suit and the
mincing woman with the big hair, who squinted up at the
sun as if she had not been outdoors in years.

Gomer bore three children in short order—two boys and
a girl who may or may not have been Hosea's—all of them
with names that only God could have picked out for them.
The oldest boy was called Jezreel, which was not so bad, except that it was the name of the town where God had promised to put an end to Israel. The middle child, a girl, was
named Not Pitied, and the baby boy got the worst one of all:

Not My People. Can you imagine? "Not My People, it's time for supper! Jezreel, have you seen Not Pitied? Children! It's time to come home now!" They were dismal names, the bitter offspring of a bitter marriage, which made Hosea's whole family a kind of poster family for God's disappointment with Israel.

After hundreds and hundreds of years of living in covenant with Yahweh, Israel still had not gotten the hang of it. She was fine as long as everything was going her way. As long as Yahweh produced good weather and fat, healthy flocks, she was content to honor her vows and stay at home, but the moment the rains failed or the cows ran low on milk, she was gone, leaving nothing but a note on the kitchen table: "Gone to see if I can't do better than this."

Where did she go? To other lovers, who promised her everything her heart desired. To Ba'al, the god of the Canaanites, the god of thunderstorms and fertility whose cult involved lots and lots of ritual writhing around. With Ba'al, there was no dreary talk of commitment or honor, no Where-were-you-last-night? and Have-you-thought-about-what-this-is-doing-to-the-children? Everything was spontaneous. You did what you felt like doing when you felt like doing it, and the only rule was to do what felt best at the time. No one knew your name and you did not know anyone else's, but it did not matter. All that mattered was giving in to the sweet, hot pulse of life.

Israel always came home again, once she had taken the edge off her appetite, once she had been reminded for the umpteenth time that the grass on the other side was never as green as it looked. One morning Yahweh would hear the screen door slam and he would smell her before he saw her: cigarette butts, musty sheets, stale beer. Then she would come into the room and lean against the door jamb looking at him, a cut on her upper lip and the fading bruise of someone's strong grip on her arm, home to the husband who took her by the hand and drew her bath and tugged her torn clothes over her head while she held her skinny arms up for him like a child.

51

She was so sorry. She would never do it again. She was through with all of that forever—but of course she was not and he knew she was not. It was just a matter of taking care of her until she got her strength back and then she would be gone again, leaving him with the groceries and the laundry and the kids and the bills until she wore herself out and wandered back to him again.

It had happened over and over, until his heart was running on empty. He had entered into covenant with her. He had promised himself to her forever and it was a promise he meant to keep, but how long could he hold up both ends of it? What would it take, to get her attention, to change her ways? Should he shake her until she came to her senses? Should he lock her in her room? Or should he divorce her and send her packing right now, before she had the chance to shame him again?

The problem was that Israel could not see herself. She could not see what she was doing, so God elected Hosea to act it all out for her, turning the prophet's life with Gomer into a parable of God's own life with Israel. "This is what it is like for me," God says to Israel through Hosea and Gomer. "If you want to know how you are acting, look at her, and tell me what you see."

Some people don't like God being the upright man in this story and Israel the no-count woman, but we all know it can go both ways. Sometimes it is the man who cannot stay home and the woman who waits there is most like God. So do not let Hosea's pronouns stop your ears. This is a marriage we are talking about. Neuter pronouns will not do. It is the marriage that is interesting—that God would choose a marriage to reveal the nature of his commitment to humankind. God could have likened it to the bond between a queen and her vassal, after all, or that of a chieftain and his ally. God could have compared it to any of the political, social, or economic covenants that were common in Hosea's time, but God did not. God chose a covenant of love instead, the most intimate of bonds, in which both partners surrender their defenses and run the risk of being hurt.

As an ordained person, I have been called upon to take part in quite a few weddings, and I confess that, on the whole, I hate them. Maybe it is because I get the feeling I am being rented, along with the tuxedos and the champagne flutes, or maybe it is because I am jealous of the bride, but I think it is because there is so much attention being lavished on the wedding and so little on the marriage. A couple who balks at spending three hours with a minister talking about their relationship thinks nothing of spending the same amount of time with the caterer or the photographer.

I suppose it is inevitable, in a culture that is so in love with love. From January until June, the checkout lines at the grocery store are waist-high in brides' magazines. Come April, florists put wedding gowns in their shop windows and society page editors start to work overtime. A wedding becomes a grand occasion for announcing one's lovability to the world at large, and who would begrudge anyone the pleasure of that?

I do not. I really do not. It is just that I know something about romance and I know something about covenant and I know which one is more likely to last. Romance is splendid. There is no doubt about it. To find someone whose sentences you can finish, whose touch makes you dizzy, who looks at you and sees the person you have always hoped you would turn out to be—that is as good as it gets. Romance is pure gift, the kind of love you do not have to work at. It happens, that is all, like a cool shower on a hot summer's night. All you have to do is have the good sense to stay out in it, opening your arms and turning your face to the sky.

A covenant, on the other hand, does not just happen. It is entered into very deliberately—a conscious act by two people who mean to make a life together. It includes promises and limits. It binds and it frees. It may begin with romance but it does not end there. After the shower is over, covenant partners start to plan the garden, disagreeing about where to put the asparagus and whether to spray the tomatoes this year.

Rarely do two people know what they are getting into when they enter a covenant, however deliberate they are. "I will love you forever no matter what." Who in their right minds believe that? And yet that is what people promise each other when they marry: not love that happens but love that lasts, a doing unto one another more than a feeling for one another, a partnership based on mutual service and trust.

When I married eleven years ago, I remember being amused by all the advice I received. "Never let the sun go down on your anger." "Don't wear old t-shirts to bed." "Always be the first one to say you're sorry." The one that puzzled me most at the time was, "The secret of a happy marriage is for both of you to give one hundred percent." Why one hundred? I thought. Why not fifty? Wouldn't it work just as well if we both gave fifty? Eleven years later, I understand. There are times when your grip just fails and the other person has to do all the holding on for both of you. Then you get a second wind and it is your turn to hold on, while your partner scrambles to get back on board.

Hosea knew that from his wedding day on. He started out giving one hundred percent and he kept it up, until one day word reached him that Gomer had sold herself back to the house where he had found her. She had abandoned the covenant, and it looked as if he might be free to wash his hands of her at last. The only problem was that his life with Gomer was all wrapped up with Yahweh's life with Israel, and Yahweh was not done yet. "I will hedge up her way with thorns," Yahweh threatened his own unfaithful spouse. "I will build a wall against her. I will uncover her lewdness in the sight of her lovers, and none shall rescue her out of my hand." Hell hath no fury like a deity scorned, only this particular deity has always had a soft spot for his beloved, which says more about him than it says about her. He has a heart that just will not stop—a covenanted heart that opens to her again and again, though hers shows no sign of opening back.

"Therefore, I will now allure her, and bring her into the wilderness, and speak tenderly to her," Yahweh says, in an about-face that would give any ordinary mortal a bad case of whiplash. "From there I will give her her vineyards, and make the Valley of Achor a door of hope. There she shall respond as in the days of her youth, as at the time when she came out of the land of Egypt" (Hosea 3:14-15). It is a remarkable speech, as if God had said, "Given all my choices—including but not limited to punishment, banishment, coercion, divorce—I choose to keep covenant. I choose love."

Israel had no right to expect treatment like that. She had brought nothing but grief to the covenant. She had not kept up her end of the bargain, but God's promise is grounded in grace, not bargains, and God's covenant lasts forever. What follows, in the second chapter of Hosea, is a renewal of vows. The invited guests include the beasts of the field, the birds of the air, and the creeping things of the ground, as God revives the covenant with all creation.

The ritual includes the breaking of bows and arrows, the snapping of a sword across the groom's bended knee. "I will make you lie down in safety," the groom says to his troublesome bride, "and I will betroth you to me forever; I will betroth you to me in righteousness and in justice, in steadfast love, and in mercy. I will betroth you to me in faithfulness, and you shall know the Lord."

They are not very romantic vows. Who lies awake at night dreaming of a just and righteous lover? Who looks for a merciful spouse? God does, apparently, and by doing so God teaches Israel to do the same thing. These are the qualities that last, God reminds her. These are the dowry I offer for your love. I ask nothing in return. The vows are all mine. Just stay home so I can love you. That is really all I ask.

Then, to seal the covenant, Yahweh calls the children to him and changes their names. Jezreel shall no longer mean the place of destruction. It shall mean, "God Sows." Henceforth, Not Pitied shall be known as "I Will Have Pity," and

Not My People shall become "You Are My People." Under the covenant, curse becomes blessing and threat blossoms into hope. All things are made new by this new exchange of vows, only nothing has been exchanged, as yet. The moment of truth is yet to come.

"You are my people," God says, face to face with his bride. Here is half the promise, God's hand held out, palm up. It is a gesture that longs for response, half a sentence that only Israel can finish. "You are my people," God says to her, and the whole earth holds its breath while she studies the hand held out to her. She studies it and then she closes her eyes, humming to herself as she folds her arms in front of her. She shifts her weight. She taps her foot. The children are on the verge of explosion when she opens her eyes and speaks at last.

"Thou art my God," she says, reaching out to take the hand that has been offered her, and all the beasts of the field and the birds of the air, all the creeping things of the ground and the leaping children converge in a pandemonium of delight.

Meanwhile, across town, the same thing has happened at Hosea and Gomer's house. Fed up with waiting for her to come home to him, he has gone and found her, and bought her back from the people she sold herself to, and pledged himself to her again. And from that day on, there was no more gossip about Gomer in town.

Blood Covenant

Then he took a cup, and after giving thanks he gave it to them, saying, "Drink from it, all of you; for this is my blood of the covenant, which is poured out for many for the forgiveness of sins." (Matthew 26:27-28)

WHEN I WAS eight years old, Mary Perkins and I decided to become blood sisters. We each had sisters of our own, but our love for them paled next to our love for one another. We were partners. Together we had jammed water sprinklers on the golf course, hanging underneath a wooden footbridge like bats while the guard rode over it in his golf cart looking for us. We were hot on the trail of a villain named the Black Dagger Man who we believed was causing much more serious mischief in our neighborhood. We never actually saw him, but that was the summer we were reading Nancy Drew mysteries to each other and we knew that there were villains everywhere, especially where you least expected them. We were also community-minded. We were disturbed by the sudden proliferation of blinking neon lights in the village where we lived, so we launched a campaign called "Help Stamp Out Nervous Neon Lights," although as far as I know we were the only two advocates of it.

Finally we decided to cement our relationship by exchanging blood. I do not remember where we got the idea, but we were very scrupulous about it. Mary borrowed a needle from her mother's sewing basket, I lifted a matchbook from my father's bureau, and we met in the woods behind the post office at high noon on a Saturday. First we sterilized the needle over the flame of a match, then we held out the forefingers of our right hands and swore to be loyal to each other forever. Whenever one of us hollered for help, the other would drop whatever she was doing and come running. We would rescue each other. We would defend each other. We would love each other above all others.

After we had solemnly promised these things, I drove the needle into my finger and handed it to Mary, who did the same thing to hers. Each of us squeezed our wounds until a little bead of blood trembled on the ends of our fingers. Then we pressed them together—hard—and grinned at each other over the bridge we had made, imagining we felt the tingle of each other's blood in our veins.

In the era of AIDS, this is not as winsome a ritual as it once was. The exchange of blood bespeaks contagion, not relation, although we must still risk it, the Red Cross tells us, if lives are to be saved. Whether the purpose is saving lives or kinship, however, the ritual of blood covenant has been going on a long, long time. There is evidence of it on every continent in the world in places as far apart in every way as Borneo and Scandinavia, evidence preserved in folklore and legend as well as in the memory of tribal people who have remained close to their roots.

Not too long ago I spent a day in the library reading up on covenant. As I was browsing the modern commentaries, I spied an old, leatherbound volume parked between them. The title had been rubbed off years before, but the gold embossed image on the cover remained: two intertwined human forearms, each spouting a fountain of blood, and just underneath them, a chalice into which their combined juices flowed. It was *The Blood Covenant*, published in 1855 by H. Clay Trumbull, who had tracked blood kinship all over the world. One story he told concerned a friend of his who had just returned from the mountains of Lebanon, where he had observed a blood covenant between two young men of ancient Arab descent. This is how it went:

First the young men met at an open place in front of the village fountain, where they were surrounded by the relatives and neighbors they had invited to witness their covenant. Then they declared their purpose to the crowd—to become each other's closest kin—and they spelled out what that would mean for each of them while a scribe copied down what they said, not once but twice, so that each man would have a record of the promises he had made. After that was done, both men signed both copies of the covenant paper along with several of their witnesses, and together they moved to the center of the crowd.

Then one friend took a sharp lancet and opened a vein in the other's arm, inserted a hollow quill into the wound and drank the living blood of his friend. When he was through, he wiped the lancet on one set of the covenant papers and stood still while his friend repeated the whole procedure on him. Then both men declared in unison, "We are brothers in a covenant made before God: who deceiveth the other, him God will deceive."

Then both of the bloodstained covenant papers were folded into one-inch squares and sewn into matching leather amulets that the young men would wear around their necks for the rest of their lives, a token of their indissoluble union. As brothers of the covenant, they had forged a bond between themselves that was more sacred than any other bond in their lives, including parentage and marriage. From that day forth, neither of them lived for himself alone. Each was possessor of a double life, having taken his friend's life and nature into himself.

I have often thought that the divorce rate in this country would plummet if blood covenant became a required part of the marriage ceremony. Actually, the marriage rate would plummet, because while large numbers of us can work up the nerve to pledge our lifelong love to one another, the idea of backing that up with a little flesh and blood takes more courage than most of us have. The blood test alone has been known to fell an otherwise sturdy groom, but still you have to admire those Lebanese blood brothers. Now *that* is a covenant!

Belief in the power of shared blood must come from some place way down deep inside of us, because it shows up over and over again in the stories that have shaped our sensibilities. In the romances of King Arthur, for instance, there is a story about a maiden daughter of King Pellinore—Percival's sister—who accompanied her brother and Sir Galahad to a distant castle in search of the Holy Grail.

When they drew near the place, a band of knights from the castle accosted them and told them the custom in that land. Every maiden who passed through it had to yield a dish full of her blood. Percival and Galahad would hear nothing of it and slew a bunch of the knights in defense of their fair maiden. It was not until they made their way to the castle that they learned the rest of the story.

Inside the castle a noble lady lay sick unto death, and the only way she could be saved was to be anointed with the blood of a pure maiden who was also a king's daughter. Hearing this, Percival's sister agreed at once to give her blood, but she gave so much that it killed her. "I die, brother," she said, wilting in front of him, "for the healing of this lady."

In all of these stories, blood is the vehicle of transferred life. Like rising sap, like a bubbling spring, it contains the very essence of life and because it does, it is a direct link to the divine source of all life. When Cain kills Abel, his brother's blood cries out to God from the ground on which it was spilled. When Noah comes stumbling down the gangplank of the ark, the first thing he does is to make a blood offering in thanksgiving to God. Abraham, too, sacrifices five animals as part of his covenant with God. Moses throws blood on the altar and on the people when he gives them the book of the law. Every male child who is circumcised sheds blood in the name of the covenant, and God is very clear that blood is precious stuff—not just human blood but animal blood as well—because the blood of a creature is its life, and that makes it sacred to the author of all life.

"Then what about the lives of all those poor sacrificial animals?" That is what you want to know, right? All I can tell you is what I have been told: that in the ancient world, blood had everlasting life in it, life that outlived its temporary host, and it was the sharing of the blood that mattered—the offering of it—whether it was your own blood or the substitute blood of the most perfect animal you could find. The death of the creature was not important. It was a means to an end, and the end glorified the means. In its death, the creature made life possible for another—much as Percival's sister did—and its death was swallowed up in life. This is very hard stuff for us moderns. There are not many of us who do butchering anymore, much less sacrificial butchering, and the shedding of blood is something we work hard to stop. We hear the story of Abraham and Isaac and we want to yell, "Stop! Take that boy back down the hill, old man! What in the world do you think you are doing?" The only reason we repeat the story at all is because it turned out all right in the end—that is, it turned out the way we wanted it to, because we cannot fathom Abraham's willingness to go as far as he did with his son. But in his world, it was the covenant with God that mattered. If he broke that, his son's life would be worth nothing to him. By offering God his only son, he offered the one thing he had to give that was more precious to him than himself. Killing Isaac was not the point; sharing Isaac's life blood was, and while we thank God it did not come to that, what do we think we are doing when we come to the Lord's supper?

"Take, eat, this is my body," Jesus said. Then he took the cup, and when he had given thanks he gave it to them, saying, "Drink of it, all of you; for this is my blood of the new covenant, which is poured out for many for the forgiveness of sins." Have we done it so often that we have forgotten how to be shocked by it? Of course it is not real blood in the cup. It is probably Taylor's Tawny Port, but clearly, this is a blood covenant we are being asked to enter into, with staggering implications.

While we tend to keep children away from it until they "understand" what they are doing, most of them understand it better than we do. Try offering a child her first communion. Hold the silver cup down where she can reach it. Watch her peer inside, sniffing the sweet, heavy stuff. Her hands come up to take the chalice. "The blood of Christ," you say, thinking how well this is going, how touching it all is. "Yuck!" she says, jerking away like she has been stung. "I don't want any!"

Would any of us, if it were the real thing? And yet it was a real thing that happened on that hill outside of Jerusalem, something utterly beyond our comprehension involving the gift of life's blood that bound us to God in a whole new way. No one stuck a hollow quill in anyone else's vein. No vows were recorded, no amulets made. There was nothing written down anywhere except over his head: "This is Jesus, the King of the Jews." But when it was all over, the world was a different place, and the world knew it. The earth shook. Rocks split. Tombs groaned and fell open to the light.

A new covenant was in effect—one Jeremiah had talked about hundreds of years before without knowing how it would come to pass. Now it had, and no one could have predicted it, that God should become flesh and blood in order to bring divine love to life, that God should become it and then give it up, so there could be no further doubt about God's faithfulness to the covenant.

It was a covenant in which God agreed to do everything. There would be no more waiting around for humankind to wise up and obey, no more temper tantrums when they did not, no more elaborate systems of punishment and reward. All God had ever wanted to do was to save their stubborn hides so that God could love them, but with the new covenant all of that was over. "Here," God said with the gift of a son—the one thing God had to give that was more precious to him than himself. "You don't have to come to me where I am anymore. I will come all the way to you where you are, through this beloved child."

And the child was willing. He was not forced to do what he did. He chose it—not easily, not without almost dying of sorrow first, but he chose it. No one forced his hand when he broke that bread. No one made him raise that cup. "Drink of it, all of you, for this is my blood of the new covenant, which is poured out for many for the forgiveness of sins."

It is important, I think, that Judas was there that night. Knowing what Judas would do, Jesus did not bar him from the table. He set a place for him, he ordered food for him, he ate out of the same dish with him. Judas was included until he excluded himself, which gives this new covenant some real bite. When Jesus holds up the cup and offers what is in it as the fluid of forgiveness, he is not talking to people with a short list of minor sins. He is talking to people who will turn him in, who will scatter to the four winds at the first sign of trouble, and who will swear they never knew him. He is talking to people who should have been his best friends on earth, who will turn out not to have a loyal bone in their bodies, and he is forgiving them ahead of time, as surely as if he had said, "I know who you are. I know you will not be innocent of the blood in this cup, but I will not let that come between us. Look, here, I bless it. I make it my gift to you. Let it mean life to you, not death. Let my life become your life, through the blood of this covenant."

"I die, brother, for the healing of this lady."

"I die, father, for the healing of this people."

The death cannot be overlooked, nor should it be, but it is the life that is being offered, the life that rushes out of that cup like a spring of living water. It is God's promise from before time and forever, spelled out this time in flesh and blood. It is the new covenant and the last one—new because it is offered to us fresh each day and last because there is nothing more that God can say or do. This is as close as God can get: blood kin, indissoluble union, friend bound to friend for life, forever. When we lift the cup to our lips and drink, we accept the gift, renewing the covenant and reminding ourselves that we do not live for ourselves alone. We are possessors of a double life, having taken our friend's life and nature into ourselves. Inside of us God rides our bloodstreams straight to our hearts where the covenant is written: I shall be your God and you shall be my people.

Absence

The Silence of God

Is not this the fast that I choose: to loose the bonds of injustice, to undo the thongs of the yoke, to let the oppressed go free, and to break every yoke? Is it not to share your bread with the hungry, and bring the homeless poor into your house; when you see the naked, to cover them, and not to hide yourself from your own kin? (Isaiah 58:6-7)

ALMOST EVERYONE HAS a story to tell about the first time God let you down. Maybe you were eight, or ten, or twenty. You did everything right, just the way you had been taught. You knelt by your bed, you clasped your hands in front of you, and you prayed for all you were worth. You gave yourself away; you held nothing back. You asked God for a sign, a hand, a map, a cure, and you waited, confidently, for God's answer to your prayer. Only it never came. Your need was not addressed, not directly, and you either learned to pray another way or else you gave it up altogether, because God turned out to be more stubborn than you had thought—more stubborn or more distant, but in either case, not who you had thought.

"Why do we fast, but you do not see?" God's people ask in the fifty-eighth chapter of Isaiah. "Why humble ourselves, but you do not notice?" It is not just an individual complaint; it is a human complaint that affects our lives in community as well as our lives at home. "Why do we worship, but you do not reveal yourself to us? Why do we pray, Sunday after Sunday, for peace, for health, for safety, but you do not give us those things? Why is the world so far from our desires for it, and why don't you speak—loudly and clearly—so the whole world can hear?"

God's silence is stunning, especially for those of us who talk a lot. We think, perhaps, that we can solve the problem by making more noise ourselves, but it is only when we stop, and hush, that the silence can teach us anything: namely, that our disillusionment is not a bad thing. Take the word apart and you can begin to hear what it really means. Dis-il-lusion-ment. The loss of illusion. The end of make-believe. Is that a bad thing? Or a good thing? To learn that God's presence is not something we can demand, that God's job is not to reward our devotion, that God's agenda may in fact be quite different from our own. Is that a bad thing or a good thing to know?

"Announce to my people their rebellion," God says to the prophet Isaiah, "to the house of Jacob their sins. Yet day after day they seek me and delight to know my ways, as if they were a nation that practiced righteousness and did not forsake the ordinance of their God" (Isaiah 58:1-2). That is how God answered the chosen people when they wanted to know where he had gone, and it is one of those answers that makes you wish for the silence again. "It is not I who have forsaken you," God says to the people, "but you who have forsaken me. If you cannot hear me, it is because you have strayed far from my voice. It is not I who am ignoring you, but you who are ignoring me."

The big disillusionment for the chosen people was that God was not where they thought. They thought God was supposed to be with them when they prayed and fasted and studied their scriptures. They thought nothing pleased God more than to find them on their knees, dressed in sackcloth and covered with ashes—but they were wrong.

God was not at their prayer desks with them. God was out in the streets, warming his hands over a can of burning garbage with a bunch of drifters, delivering sacks of groceries down at the housing project, handing out blankets to those who slept shivering in the bushes. God was not parked in their sanctuaries, waiting for one of them to stop by for a talk. God was in the emergency room at the city hospital, in the waiting room at the labor pool, in the lobby at the police station, not only to comfort those who were stuck there but also to stir them up—reminding them of their birthright, their inherent nobility; reminding them that they were the long-lost sons and daughters of heavenly royalty, who were meant for more excellent lives.

"Is not this the fast that I choose," God said to the sackcloth and ashes crowd, "to loose the bonds of injustice, to undo the thongs of the yoke, to let the oppressed go free, to break every yoke?" The big disillusionment for the chosen people was that they could not serve God without serving their neighbors. Their relationship to God was not separable from their relationship to other people, especially the least of them. They had hoped they could keep their faith a private matter between them and their God, but it turned out to be an illusion.

"It is a great mistake to suppose that God is chiefly interested in religion," wrote an archbishop of the last century, and Isaiah seems to agree. God is not interested in religion; God is interested in human beings, and particularly in the demolition of our illusions: that we can hold ourselves apart from one another, that we are not related to one another, that some people are simply destined to be winners and others to be losers and that there is nothing to be done about it, except perhaps to build some walls and install some security systems and relocate some neighborhoods in order to keep the one from spilling over into the other.

"Will you call this a fast, a day acceptable to the Lord?"

I am guilty. Ten months ago, I relocated my neighborhood, leaving the big city of Atlanta for a little town in North Georgia. I left because it was time for a change, but I also left because I was tired of being afraid all the time, and locking my doors all the time, and defending myself against people I was called to serve. Not the ones inside the church. I did all right with them. It was the ones outside the church who spooked me: the men who congregated in the parking lot late at night with bottles in paper bags; the women who hurled abuse at the receptionist for giving them one more telephone number to call instead of the help they needed;

the children who clung to their mothers' legs with eyes one hundred years old. They were only the tip of the iceberg, and I knew it. I knew the city was full of catacombs where people existed on very little light and air, where bullets flew and babies' stomachs growled and old people froze to death in their beds because they could not pay their utility bills.

So I left. I had an illusion that the country would be different, and for the first few weeks it was. All I saw were the cows, and the clouds, and the fields full of wildflowers. But once I had gotten used to those, I started seeing other things: the Mexican children playing in the drainage ditch at the trailer park, the Laotian women coming out of the chicken processing plant with their hair in white nets, the old folks at the grocery store with almost nothing in their carts, trying to decide between beans and cereal for supper. I had an illusion that the country would be different, but God disillusioned me.

Hiding ourselves from our kin is not a city issue or a rural issue but a human issue, and living with the fact of it is like living with a sore that will not heal. Everywhere you turn, it hurts. In order to hide from your brothers and sisters, you have to avert your gaze a lot. You have to learn when to look and when not to look. You have to plan your routes through town very carefully. Tinting your windows helps, or wearing dark glasses. Better yet, stay home altogether, or live somewhere with a guard at the gate. We can do that. That is one of our choices, but if we do, then we should not be surprised when we ring God and get no answer, or leave a message that is never returned, because we cannot hide ourselves from our kin without hiding ourselves from God. Isn't that a kick in the pants? We cannot defend ourselves against each other without defending ourselves against God.

A couple of years ago I decided to use public transportation whenever I could. It was an environmental commitment, at that point; I had not really thought about the social consequences, most of which became clear to me the first time I boarded a Greyhound bus for Augusta. I was the only middle class white lady aboard that day, and while I settled myself in my seat with my Walkman and my theological journals, my fellow passengers greeted each other loudly and started spreading their belongings around. Once we got underway, it was like a block party on wheels. People asked each other their names and tried to figure out if they knew any of the same people in Augusta. They passed fried chicken around and fell asleep on each other's shoulders. They held each other's screaming babies and traded stories that made them howl with laughter, while the middle class white lady, sitting up front all by herself, turned up the volume on her Walkman and read about the kingdom of God.

God has given us another way, a way as old as Isaiah and as up-to-date as the evening news. We can surrender our illusions of separateness, of safety and superiority. We can leave our various sanctuaries and seek God where God may be found, gathering in the streets—or in the Greyhound bus station—to figure out how to untie the fancy knots of injustice and how to take the yokes of oppression apart. We can pool our resources so that the hungry have bread and the homeless have houses and the naked have something to cover their shame. Above all, we can learn to claim our own kin, asking them what their names are, telling them our own, and refusing to hide from them anymore. "Then your light shall break forth like the dawn," says the Lord, "and your healing shall spring up quickly. Then you shall call, and the Lord will answer; you shall cry for help, and he will say, Here I am" (Isaiah 58:8-9).

If God is silent, it may be because we are not speaking God's language yet, but there is still time. God has taught us how to break the silence and has even given us the words. "Here I am." They are the words we long to hear, but they are also the words God longs for us to speak—to stand before a sister, a brother, and say, "Here I am."

Those of us who decide to try it should listen real hard when we are through, because there is likely to be an echo in the air—not silence anymore, but the very voice of God, saying, "Yes. Hello. Welcome home. Here I am. Here I am."

Looking Up
Toward Heaven

When Jesus had said this, as they were watching, he was lifted up, and a cloud took him out of their sight. (Acts 1:9)

ON SUNDAY MORNINGS a great division takes place among American people, as some go to church and most stay home. Those who stay home are not taking a week off; church is simply not part of their lives. As far as they are concerned, houses of worship are little more than pretty antiques, fussed over by wishful thinkers who do not know when to admit they are wrong and go home. It is one of the most peculiar things twentieth-century human beings can do, to come together week after week with no intention of being useful or productive, but only of facing an ornate wall to declare things they cannot prove about a God they cannot see.

Our word for it is worship and it is hard to justify in this day and age, but those of us who do it over and over again begin to count on it. This is how we learn where we fit. This is how we locate ourselves between the past and the future, between our hopes and our fears, between the earth and the stars. This is how we learn who we are and what we are supposed to be doing: by coming together to sing and to pray, to be silent and to be still, by peering into the darkness together and telling each other what we see when we do. We may baffle our unbelieving friends and neighbors, but it cannot be helped. Half the time we baffle ourselves, proclaiming good news when the news is so bad, trusting the light when the sky is so dark, continuing to wait on the savior in our midst when all the evidence suggests that he packed up and left a long, long time ago.

To be theologically correct, we have been waiting ever since the first Ascension Day, when Jesus led his disciples to a mount called Olivet just outside of Jerusalem, spoke to them for the last time, and disappeared inside a cloud for good. You can read about it in the first chapter of the book of Acts, how one moment he was there with them and the next moment he was gone, his well-known hand raised in final blessing, his face grown bright and indistinct, his familiar shape vanishing into the fog like the end of a dream too good to be true—all of it slipping out of their reach until he was no longer there for them, no longer present but past, a memory that would haunt them to the end of their days.

Where he went, according to tradition, was to heaven— which may not be up, exactly, as much as it is beyond—and what he went there to do was to finish what he had begun with us. It was not enough that through him God was born into the body of the world; that was just his Christmas gift to us. His ascension gift was that through him the body of the world was borne back to God. By presenting his own ruined, risen body to be seated at the right hand of God, Jesus imported flesh and blood into those holy precincts for the first time. He paved the way for us, so that when we arrive there later everyone will not be quite so shocked by us. He restored the goodness of creation, and ours in particular. By ascending bodily into heaven, he showed us that flesh and blood are good, not bad; that they are good enough for Jesus, good enough for heaven, good enough for God. By putting them on and keeping them on, Jesus has not only brought God to us; he has also brought us to God.

I tried all of that out on a friend last week. "Isn't that incredible?" I said. "Doesn't that make the ascension come alive for you?"

"Interesting," he said, "but not compelling."

What he meant, I think, is that it is still an abstract idea—an explanation that has very little to do with our day-to-day experience. Almost everything else that happened to Jesus makes sense in terms of my own life. He was born to a human mother; so was I. He ate and drank and slept at night; so do I. He loved people and got angry with people and forgave people; so have I. He wept; me too. He died; I will die too. He rose from the dead; I even know something about that. I have had some Easter mornings of my own— joy found in the midst of sorrow, life in the midst of death.

But ascending into heaven to be seated at the right hand of God? That is where Jesus and I part company. That is where he leaves me in the dust. My only experience of the ascension is from the ground, my neck cranked back as far as it will go, my mouth wide open, my face shielded from the sun by the cloud that is bearing my Lord away.

Luke ends his gospel by telling us that the disciples returned to Jerusalem with great joy, and I expect that is true. But you have to remember that it had just happened for them, that they had just been with him, and the memory was fresh. They were still running on adrenaline; you can see it in the pictures. Almost every church with stained glass windows has an ascension window tucked away somewhere. In it, Christ generally hovers in the air, his hands upraised in blessing, while the disciples look up at him with something between awe and delight. But he is there with them—*he is in the window*—and if they went away joyful then I cannot help thinking that it was because they thought he would be back in a day or two, next week at the latest.

Two thousand years later, we tend to see the whole thing a little differently. We need a new window to describe our own situation: a window with just us in it—no angels, no Jesus, no heavenly light—just us, still waiting, still watching the sky, our faces turned up like empty cups that only one presence can fill. But he is not present anymore, not the way he used to be. Ascension Day is the day the present Lord became absent, which may be why it is the most forgotten feast day of the church year. Who wants to celebrate being left behind? Who wants to mark the day that Jesus went out of this world, never to be seen again? Hungry as we are for the presence of God, the one thing we do *not* need is a day to remind us of God's absence.

Or is that really the one reason, underneath all the other reasons, we are here? Because we have sensed God's absence—in our hollow nights, our pounding hearts, our unanswered prayers—and because those things have not discouraged us from coming here but have in fact brought us here, to seek the presence we have been missing?

Sometimes I think absence is underrated. It is not *nothing*, after all. It is something: a heightened awareness, a sharpened appetite, a finer perception. When someone important to me is absent from me, I become clearer than ever what that person means to me. Details that got lost in our togetherness are recalled in our apartness, and their sudden clarity has the power to pry my heart right open. I see the virtues I have overlooked, the opportunities I have missed. The quirks that drove me crazy at close range become endearing at a distance. From that enlarged perspective, I can see that they are the very things that make my someone *someone* and not just anyone.

There is something else that happens during an absence. If the relationship is strong and true, the absent one has a way of becoming present—if not in body, then in mind and spirit.

My husband Edward is devoted to hawks, and especially to the golden eagles that are coming back to our part of Georgia. Driving down the highway with him can become a test of nerve as he cranes over the steering wheel to peer at the wing feathers of a particularly large bird. Is it an eagle? Or just a turkey vulture? He has to know, even if it means weaving down the road for a while, or running off it from time to time.

"Keep your eyes on the road!" I yell at him. "Who cares what it is? I'll buy you a bird book; I'll buy you a bird. Just watch where you're going." Then a couple of summers ago we spent two months apart and I thought I would get a break from hawks, but instead I began to see them everywhere—loping through the air, spiraling in rising thermals, hunkered down in the tops of trees. Seeing them, really *seeing* them for the first time in my life, I understood that I was not seeing them with my own eyes but with Edward's eyes. He was not there, so I was seeing them for him. He was absent—or was he? He was present in me.

One thing is for sure: there is no sense of absence where there has been no sense of presence. What makes absence hurt, what makes it ache, is the memory of what used to be there but is no longer. Absence is the arm flung across the bed in the middle of the night, the empty space where a beloved sleeper once lay. Absence is the child's room now empty and hung with silence and dust. Absence is the overgrown lot where the old house once stood, the house in which people laughed and thought their happiness would last forever.

You cannot miss what you have never known, which makes our sense of absence—and especially our sense of God's absence—the very best proof that we knew God once, and that we may know God again. There is loss in absence, but there is also hope, because what happened once can happen again and only an empty cup can be filled. It is only when we pull that cup out of hiding, when we own up to the emptiness, the absence, the longing inside—it is only then that things can begin to change.

It is our sense of God's absence, after all, that brings us to church in search of God's presence. Like a band of forlorn disciples, we return to this hillside again and again. It is the place we lost track of him; it is the last place we saw him, so of course it is the first place anybody thinks to look for him to come again. We have been coming here a long time now, but even in his absence it is a good place to remember him—to recall best moments and argue about the details, to swap all the old stories until they begin to revive again, the life flowing back into them like feeling into a numb limb. It hurts at first, but then it is fine, and the joy of remembering makes the pain seem a small price to pay.

"Men of Galilee, why do you stand looking up toward heaven?" That is what the two men in white robes said to the disciples on the mount called Olivet just outside of Jerusalem. Luke calls them men in white robes, anyway, so as not to scare anyone, but you can bet your last nickel that they were angels—angels sent to remind God's friends that if they wanted to see him again, it was no use looking up. Better they should look around instead, at each other, at the world, at the ordinary people in their ordinary lives, because that was where they were most likely to find him—not the way they used to know him, but the new way, not in his own body but in their bodies, the risen, the ascended Lord who was no longer anywhere on earth so that he could be everywhere instead.

No one standing around watching them that day could have guessed what an astounding thing happened when they all stopped looking into the sky and looked at each other instead. On the surface, it was not a great moment: eleven abandoned disciples with nothing to show for all their following. But in the days and years to come it would become very apparent what had happened to them. With nothing but a promise and a prayer, those eleven people consented to become the church and nothing was ever the same again, beginning with them. The followers became leaders, the listeners became preachers, the converts became missionaries, the healed became healers. The disciples became apostles, witnesses of the risen Lord by the power of the Holy Spirit, and nothing was ever the same again. That probably was not the way they would have planned it. If they had had it their way, they would probably have tied Jesus up so that he could not have gotten away from them, so that they would have known where to find him and rely on him forever. Only that is not how it happened. He went away—he was *taken* away—and they stood looking up toward heaven. Then they stopped looking up toward heaven, looked at each other instead, and got on with the business of being the church.

And once they did that, surprising things began to happen. They began to say things that sounded like him, and they began to do things they had never seen anyone but him do before. They became brave and capable and wise. Whenever two or three of them got together it was always as if there were someone else in the room with them whom they could not see—the strong, abiding presence of the absent one, as available to them as bread and wine, as familiar to them as each other's faces. It was almost as if he had not ascended but exploded, so that all the holiness that was once concentrated in him alone flew everywhere, flew far and wide, so that the seeds of heaven were sown in all the fields of the earth.

We go to church to worship, to acknowledge the Lord's absence and to seek the Lord's presence, to sing and to pray, to be silent and to be still, to hold out the empty cups of our hands and to be filled with bread, with wine, with the abiding presence of the absent Lord until he comes again. Do you miss him sometimes? Do you long for assurance that you have not been left behind? Then why do you stand looking up toward heaven? Look around you, look around.

Good News
for Orphans

Peace I leave with you; my peace I give to you. I do not give to you as the world gives. Do not let your hearts be troubled, and do not let them be afraid. You heard me say to you, "I am going away, and I am coming to you." (John 14:27-28)

IF YOU READ the gospel of John straight through, things slow to a crawl around chapter fourteen. The last supper is over. Judas has left the room like a hive of yellow jackets were after him. Everyone's feet are clean and Jesus' hands are still puckered from washing them all when he begins to talk. "Love one another, do not be afraid; believe in God, believe also in me. Where I am going you cannot follow me now, but I will not leave you orphaned. I go to prepare a place for you, and if I go and prepare a place for you, I will come again and take you to myself, so that where I am, you may be also."

He goes on like this for four whole chapters, telling his disciples everything they need to know before he leaves them. Where is he going? He is going to die, as a matter of fact. Only that is not how he tells it. The way he tells it, he is heading off to a family reunion with his father that no one else is invited to, and he is leaving them in charge while he is gone. He will be back, but meanwhile his list is so long that it raises some anxiety in them about how long he will be away. "A little while," he reassures them, "and you will see me."

A few of them did, later on, but then he was gone again. A little while became a long while. A long while became a lifetime. Ten years turned into a hundred years, then five hundred years, then a thousand. Now, from where we sit, it has been so long that some of us wonder if we have not been orphaned after all. Is he gone or isn't he? And if he is gone, where has he gone and what in the world will we do without him? And if he is not gone, where is he, exactly, and why doesn't he show himself?

As the eldest of three daughters, I was the designated babysitter in my family. From the time I was twelve, I was the one my parents left in charge when they went out at night. First my father would sit me down and remind me how much he and my mother trusted me—not only because I was the oldest but also because I was the most responsible. This always made me dizzy, but I agreed with him. I would not let the house burn down. I would not open the door to strangers. I would not let my little sisters fall down the basement steps.

Then my mother would show me where she had left the telephone number, remind me when they would be home, and all together we would walk to the front door where everyone kissed everyone good-bye. Then the lock clicked into place, and a new era began. I was *in charge*. Turning around to face my new responsibilities, what I saw were my sisters' faces, looking at me with something between hope and fear. They knew I was no substitute for what they had just lost, but since I was all they had they were willing to try.

And so was I. I played games with them, I read them books, I made them pimento cheese sandwiches on white bread with the crusts cut off. But as the night wore on they got crankier and crankier. Where are mommy and daddy? Where did they go? When will they be back? I told them over and over again. I made up elaborate stories about what we would all do together in the morning. I promised them that if they would go to sleep I would make sure mommy and daddy kissed them good night when they came in. I tried to make everything sound normal, but how did I know? Our parents might have had a terrible accident. They might never come home again and the three of us would be split apart, each of us sent to a different foster home so that we never saw each other again.

It was hard, being the babysitter, because I was a potential orphan too. I had as much to lose as my sisters, and as much to fear, but I could not give in to it because I was the one in charge. I was supposed to know better. I was supposed to exude confidence and create the same thing in them. I was supposed to know all the answers.

Plenty of you know what I mean, not only because you were babysitters too but because you are Christians. We are all of us Christ's elder children in the world, the ones he has left in charge. We are the responsible ones, the ones he has trusted to carry on in his name, and everywhere we go we see the faces of those whom he has given into our care. Some of them are still hungry to see him and some of them are not. Some of them are still open to his return and some of them have closed their hearts. Some of them are still waiting and some of them have clearly given up. At first they jumped out of bed whenever they thought they heard footsteps on the stairs, but now they know better. Morning may come and it may not. They may wait to find out and they may not, slipping off into the night to look for some other, more reliable light.

Where is he? Where did he go? And when will he be back? It is hard, being the ones in charge, because we are potential orphans too, only he said we would not be. He said he was going away, but he also said he was coming back again, and not only at the end of time.

"Those who love me will keep my word," he said before he left, "and my Father will love them, and we will come to them and make our home with them" (John 14:23). Not visit. Not pass through from time to time. Not send a postcard. "We will come to them and make our home with them." John only uses the word "home" twice in his gospel, both times around the last supper table. "In my Father's house there are many homes (or dwelling places)," Jesus says a little earlier. "I go to prepare a place for you." It is not a temporary place he is talking about but a permanent one, an abode large enough to accommodate the love that binds him to God on one hand and binds him to us on the other, a giant heart of a place with room enough for everyone whom love unites.

It is John's idea of heaven to move in with the God who has moved in with us—only the address changes between the first time he writes it down and the second. It was out there somewhere the first time, a place in the future where Jesus was going that no one could follow him to, a place we would have to wait for him to come back from and show us.

By the second time John writes it down, Jesus is no longer going but coming. The place is not out there somewhere but right here, a place in the present where God dwells with those who love Jesus and keep his word. "Abiding," he calls it, "staying put." "We will come to them and make our home with them."

I am a little fuzzy on the details, as John himself is, but abiding seems to involve becoming part of a large extended family, and a holy one at that. When God and Jesus move in with us, apparently, they make lots of keys—keys for the Holy Spirit, keys for other disciples, keys for all kinds of in-dwelling cousins in Christ. Coming and going, we learn to recognize each other, and to call upon each other for everything that people who live together do.

Whatever else this is, it is very good news for babysitters, because it means we are not alone in the house. There is someone else at home, in us and in those for whom we care, which means that we do not have to be God-sized for them. We can be human-sized instead, with room within us for God to dwell and heal all our hearts from the inside out.

It is very good news for orphans too, because we do not have to be. Those who truly love us live inside us, and no one shall snatch us out of their hands. We may have to learn a new way of communicating with them, since they are inside us now and not outside, where we can hang on to them in the old way. If we want to talk with them, we may have to sit down someplace quiet and listen very carefully for the sound of the wind blowing inside of us, for the sound of the still small voice that speaks in silence more often than it speaks in words, but henceforth there can be no doubt about where home is for them or for us. Coming or going, God dwells with us, leaving us notes all over the place: "Love one another, don't be afraid; believe in God, believe also in me. If it were not so, would I have told you?"

The First Breakfast

Gathered there together were Simon Peter, Thomas called the Twin, Nathanael of Cana in Galilee, the sons of Zebedee, and two others of his disciples. Simon Peter said to them, "I am going fishing." They said to him, "We will go with you." They went out and got into the boat, but that night they caught nothing. (John 21:2-3)

JOHN'S GOSPEL DOES not end once but twice. In the first ending, Jesus came to his disciples as they cowered behind locked doors. He breathed new life into them and sent them forth in his name. He gave them peace. John made it sound like the end, but it was not the end, or at least not the only end, because in the twenty-first chapter we have another story about Jesus and his disciples, the second ending of John's gospel. If it is all a little confusing, it is hard to blame John, because everyone knows how hard it is to come to an end. You think you have said everything, and then you think of something else, something too important to leave out. "P.S.," you write at the bottom of the page, and maybe a "P.P.S." after that, because it is hard to stop, hard to fold the letter and lick the stamp and call it done.

On the whole, human beings are not so good at endings. We are much better at beginnings, when everything is new and exciting and full of possibilities. We like to hold babies better than we like to visit nursing homes. We like daybreak better than midnight. We like saying hello better than we like saying goodbye, but it is not as if we get to choose. We have plenty of both in our lives—beginnings and endings—roughly one of each for everything that really matters to us at all. So it is hard to blame John for lingering over his ending for a while. He wanted to make sure he had said it all. He wanted to make sure he had given us everything we would need to make it through the long nights we might have to wait before our next daybreak came. He did not know how long it would be for us, but he knew how long it had been for some of the disciples, so he decided to tell us a story about them that might help us out.

It happened sometime after the first Easter, no one knows when exactly, but long enough for the disciples to have left Jerusalem and made the long trek back to Galilee. It was home for them. It was the place where everything had begun for them, which made it the natural place for them to return once it seemed that everything had come to an end. There were seven of them, John says, which means that they were already coming apart at the seams, some of them going one direction while the others went another. These seven decide to go fishing, and that makes a lot of sense. Fishing is a good excuse for thinking, after all, for just sitting quietly and letting silence do its healing work. It is a good thing to do when you want to do nothing, nothing but sit and watch your cork drift, knowing that your line is down there somewhere in the deep waters, just like you are, waiting to catch something, to hook something that will make it all worthwhile.

But fishing has added meaning for these seven, because it is their occupation—or was, before Jesus showed up. They do not fish for pleasure; they fish for a living. They do not fish with lines and hooks; they fish with big, heavy nets that smell of seaweed and dried fish scales, hauling them out of the bottom of the boat with hands that are calloused from years and years of casting and knotting and straining against the ropes. So when they decide to go fishing, it is not a decision to daydream but a decision to return to their former way of life, to go back to the only thing they know how to do without him.

He is gone, after all. They have not seen him since Jerusalem, and while that was a powerful time none of them will ever forget, it is time to get on with life. Memory is one thing, but the future is another. His life on earth may have ended, but theirs have not, and they have to do something about getting food on their tables and roofs over their heads. He is gone, and it is time for them to start looking after themselves again.

So they go fishing, each of them sunk in his own thoughts as he climbs into the old familiar boat again, one of them reaching out to steady the prow while the others step inside and take their old familiar places, swamped with *deja vu*. They have all been here before, but when? A hundred years ago or just yesterday? Maybe it was all a dream too good to be true, the way he walked up to them, and spoke to them like someone they had known all their lives so that there was no doubt what they would do when he called out to them to follow.

They should have known better than to have believed it, to have staked their lives on something that could come to such a quick and bloody end. They should have known that it would all boil down to business as usual, back to the grind, all their wild, joyful expectation reduced to grim resignation as they go back to their nets. Only it does not work. They fish all night long without catching a single thing. Time after time their nets come up empty, a perfect match for their hearts. So now what? They cannot go forward and they cannot go back. All they can do is sit in the dark and watch the sky change color as the sun rises behind the hills.

That is when they hear him. They cannot see him, but they can hear him, someone, calling out to them across the water, guessing the truth—that they have no fish—and suggesting that they try the other side of the boat. So they do, and the water begins to boil, all at once so dense with fish that some of them are pushed right out of the water, their shiny fins glinting in the morning light. It is *deja vu* again: the boats, the nets, the stranger calling out to them. It is not the end after all, or else the end has led them back to the beginning again.

"It is the Lord!" says the beloved disciple, also guessing the truth, and what has been a dismal midnight scene becomes pure daybreak pandemonium. Peter throws himself into the water, leaving the others with all the hard work. They scramble for their oars, catching him just as he reaches the beach, and what all of them arrive to find is a charcoal fire with fish on it, and bread, and Jesus their beloved cook.

"Come," he says to his wet, happy disciples, "and have breakfast." If you have ever eaten breakfast on a beach, then your imagination is already working overtime: copper-colored coals glowing in the sand, heat rising in the cold morning, wood smoke curling through your hair, fish sizzling over the low flames, the sound of the sea shushing behind you. It is a dream, all right, only a dream too good *not* to be true. He is not serving supper this time. That was the last meal of their old life together. This is the first meal of their new life together—a resurrection breakfast, prepared by the only one who knows the recipe.

I do not know why so many of Jesus' post-resurrection appearances have something to do with food, but they do. It happens twice in Luke—first on the road to Emmaus, where Jesus is made known to two of his disciples in the breaking of the bread, and then later, when he appears to them all and eats a piece of broiled fish in their presence. Then there is this meal, which is so reminiscent of that other meal by the sea of Galilee, where he took five loaves and two fishes and fed everyone in sight.

Maybe it is because eating is so necessary for life, and so is he. Or maybe it is because sharing food is what makes us human. Most other species forage alone, so that feeding is a solitary business, but human beings seem to love eating together. Even when we are stuck alone with a frozen dinner, most of us will open a magazine or turn on the television just for company. It is, at any rate, one of the clues to his presence. There is always the chance, when we are eating together, that we will discover the risen Lord in our midst.

This story is full of clues for those times when we too are marooned on the sea in the middle of night, afraid that we have come to the end of something without any idea how to begin again. In the first place, it is probably a good idea to pay attention to strangers, especially those who seem to know things about you that they really have no way of knowing. Whether they are giving you unsolicited advice about where to cast your nets or just standing there looking at you with eyes like daybreak, it is probably a good idea to pay attention to them since Jesus has a whole closet full of disguises.

Another clue that he may be somewhere around is a sudden change in fortune—not rags to riches, necessarily, since he actually seems to prefer rags to riches—but a sudden change in the way your life looks to you. One moment it looks hopeless to you and the next you see possibilities you never saw before. One moment your problems look too big to be budged and the next you discover handles on them you never knew were there before. One moment the net looks empty and the next it does not. There is something wriggling in it where there was nothing just a moment before. It may be a little or it may be a lot, but it is *alive*—a living thing where there was nothing but darkness and death before.

"It is the Lord!" That is what the beloved disciple said. How did he know? How does any of us know? By staying on the lookout, I suppose. By watching the shore, and the sky, and each other's faces. By listening real hard. By living in great expectation and refusing to believe that our nets will stay empty or our nights will last forever. For those with ears to hear, there is a voice that can turn all our dead ends into new beginnings.

"Come," that voice says, "and have breakfast."

Messengers

Ninevites and Ne'er-Do-Wells

When God saw what they did, how they turned from their evil ways, God changed his mind about the calamity that he had said he would bring upon them; and he did not do it. But this was very displeasing to Jonah, and he became angry. (Jonah 3:10–4:1)

AS FAR AS I am concerned, the book of Jonah has the best last line in the Bible: "And should I not be concerned about Ninevah," God says to Jonah, "that great city, in which there are more than a hundred and twenty thousand persons who do not know their right hand from their left, and also many animals?" The End. Isn't that great?

If it were not the end, however, I expect the next line would have been Jonah's. "No, you should *not* be concerned about Ninevah, no matter how many people and animals live there. Not only do they not know their right hands from their left; they also do not know right from wrong nor the Lord God Almighty from a hole in the ground. Wipe them out! That is what you told me you would do, and I told them. Now do it!"

Jonah is a hard guy to defend. Called by God to prophesy to Ninevah, he got on the next boat headed in the opposite direction and nearly got everyone on board killed before God sent a taxi in the form of a whale to turn Jonah around and spit him in the right direction. It was not just that Jonah was afraid to be a prophet. He might have said okay if God had sent him someplace nearby like Jericho or

Shechem, but Ninevah was simply out of the question. It was the capital of the Assyrian Empire, now known as Iraq—which was as hostile to Israel then as it is now—and sending Jonah there was like sending a nobody from Tel Aviv to tell Saddam Hussein he was going to hell. Jonah did not want any part of it: a) because he knew what usually happens to God's messengers and b) because he had no desire to participate in Ninevah's salvation. If the city was going to hell, let it. He was not going to intervene.

But God had a different idea, which Jonah finally realized he was going to be part of whether he liked it or not. So the second time God sent him to Ninevah he went, not because he had a change of heart but because he knew he had no choice. His only consolation was thinking how delicious it was going to be, pronouncing judgment on all those Ninevites. They had devastated Jewish cities and killed Jewish people. They had deported those who survived and taken them home to become their maids and gardeners. If Jonah was doomed to become their next victim, he would at least make sure he got in a few licks of his own before he went down.

I have an image of him rolling into town for a big preaching revival. He puts up his big tent, sprinkles sawdust on the ground, arranges the wooden benches. He spreads the word that there is a revival tonight, and as the time draws near he puts his big black Bible on the pulpit, tests the sound system, and waits for the crowds to arrive.

And they do—thousands of them, with their children and servants and livestock. Even the king is there, right there on the front row in his purple robes. Jonah knows how evil they all are, how richly they deserve God's judgment, and he cannot wait to get started. He pulls out his white handkerchief and clears his throat. "Yet forty days, and Ninevah shall be overthrown!" he shouts into the microphone, shaking his finger in the air.

That is it, the sum total of Jonah's prophecy in the Bible: an eight-word sermon. He might have been warming up to something considerably longer than that, but no one will ever know, because no sooner does he get that sentence out of his mouth than the whole city repents on the spot. "Yes!" they shout. "We believe!" The king orders a fast and leads them all out to change into sackcloth and ashes, and there stands Jonah all alone in his tent before he has even broken a sweat.

Meanwhile, the Ninevites cry mightily to God, God decides to spare them after all, and the revival is proclaimed a howling success. With one eight-word sermon, Jonah has accomplished more than all the other prophets put together. He has converted the biggest city in the enemy empire. He should be happy, right? But is he happy? No. He is so angry he could die. The last thing in the world Jonah wants is for the Ninevites to be spared. He wants them all to go up in smoke and, more important than that, he wants to be right. How do you suppose he felt, using up all his nerve to tell the Ninevites they have a little less than six weeks left on the face of the earth and then having God tap him on the shoulder to say, "Um, excuse me, Jonah, I changed my mind"?

Everyone in this story repents except Jonah. The Ninevites repent, God repents, even the cows and the goats repent, but Jonah does not repent. He slinks off to the outskirts of the city and hopes God will decide to destroy it after all, because he cannot accept the possibility that God's idea of justice might not coincide with his own.

There is a divine sense of humor loose in this story, however, and even Jonah's sulking cannot keep God from playing with him. While Jonah sits hunkered down in his hut, watching the city hopefully for some sign of earthquake or fire, God appoints a castor oil bush to grow up over his head and shade him from the heat of the sun. Jonah likes this very much. He likes this as much as he did not like what happened in Ninevah, but his happiness is short-lived. The next day God appoints a worm to attack the bush and Jonah once again threatens to die, as if this will ruin God's day or something.

"Is it right for you to be angry about the bush?" God asks him. It is a trick question, although Jonah does not seem to notice. If he says no, it really is not right for him to be so angry about the bush, then he is admitting that what happens to the bush or the Ninevites or to Jonah himself is really God's business, not his own, and that the job of deciding how the world should be run is already filled. And if he says yes, it *is* right for him to be angry about the bush, then he opens the way for God to compare the fate of the bush to the fate of a whole city full of people so that Jonah can, perhaps, get just a glimmer of his own pettiness. "Is it right for you to be angry about the bush?"

"Yes," Jonah says, "angry enough to die."

If you have never felt like that yourself, then you probably will not get the punch line of this story nor the one in the gospel about the laborers in the vineyard who arrived last and were paid as much as those who arrived first. Both stories poke a hard finger in the ribs of those of us who want God's mercy for ourselves and God's justice for other people. We rejoice when undeserved blessings come our way. Some of us even cook up reasons why we deserve them after all. This little castor oil bush must be because God really liked the firm tone I took with the Ninevites. How delightful! A small, unexpected bonus for my obedience.

Even when we know the blessings that come to us have been delivered to the wrong address, there are not many of us who will send them back. We thank God and quickly carry them inside, but when we look out the window and see the delivery man carrying an identical package next door, to those really unpleasant people who sit on the porch drinking beer after beer in broad daylight and whose children look like they belong on a UNICEF poster, well, we tend to resent that. Undeserved blessings are only supposed to go to the deserving, apparently.

We are such bookkeepers! And God is not! When the Ninevites repent, and the ne'er-do-wells at the end of the line get paid the same as the hard workers at the front of the line, and the people we judge most harshly receive the mercy of God, then it becomes painfully clear that there is something inherently unfair in the notion of grace. God does not keep track of things the way we do. God does not spend a lot of time deciding who is worthy and who is not, like we do.

God does not give any of us what we deserve but what we need, and it is hard—very hard—to trust God's judgment on that score. I do not know a child in the world today who appreciates the favors a parent shows toward a brother or sister. Never mind that the favored one is hurt, or sick, or lost. There is a clock and a calculator in every child's head. Spend five minutes more on his homework than her homework; hand over a nickel more to this one than to that one and you know what comes next: "That's not fair!"

No, it is not fair. It is grace, and I do truly believe that those of us who get offended by the divine distribution of it have simply forgotten who we are. We think we are the righteous prophets, sent to pronounce judgment on the scuzzy Assyrians. We think we are the diligent, sober workers who deserve more pay than the shiftless drifters who show up an hour before quitting time. That is how we see it, and we make the mistake of thinking that that is how God sees it too.

What we cannot know is that maybe—just maybe—from where God sits, we are all a mess. Some of us clean up better than others and some of us have figured out how to manage our fears by doing good works, but when you get right down to it, we are all Ninevites and ne'er-do-wells, only I do not think God would put it like that, because those are human labels full of human judgments. From where God sits, I expect we look more like hurt, sick, lost children, all of us in deep need of mercy.

Is it right for us to be angry? If Ninevah is spared, who won't shout hallelujah? And if those who show up at the end of the day open their envelopes to find a full day's pay, who will not rejoice? Only those who do not know who they are. The rest of us will be down in Ninevah at the party, whooping it up with all the other folks who do not know their right hands from their left, and also many animals.

God's Sharecroppers

When the harvest time had come, he sent his slaves to the tenants to collect his produce. But the tenants seized his slaves and beat one, killed another, and stoned another. Again he sent other slaves, more than the first; and they treated them in the same way. Finally he sent his son to them, saying, "They will respect my son." (Matthew 21:34-37)

JESUS' PARABLE OF the wicked tenants is fine as long as you hear it the way he tells it, from the viewpoint of the landowner. But listen to another parable. Once upon a time there was a rich businessman from Orlando who bought a derelict apple orchard in Clarkesville, Georgia. He pruned the trees, fertilized them, fixed up the sales shed and put a brand new hand-painted sign on the highway. Then he leased the place to a local family for less than market value with the understanding they would give him ten percent of the apples. With no business experience and high hopes of owning their own place some day, the new tenants agreed and sealed the deal with a handshake. Then the rich landowner got into his Lincoln Town Car and drove back to Florida and no one in Clarkesville ever laid eyes on him again.

The tenants loved the place like it was their own. They went out to tend the trees at dawn and they stayed out each day until after dark. They used organic pesticides. They hauled water by hand during the summer drought and when the first frost was predicted before the apples were ripe, they built small fires throughout the orchard and stoked them all night long, so that the trees stayed warm under a blanket of wood smoke.

Come October, the air smelled of applesauce. Every time the tenants took a deep breath, their mouths watered. Meanwhile, the trees were so heavy with fruit they looked like emerald ladies with too much jewelry on. It was time to harvest, and it had to be done quickly, so the tenants worked in shifts, half of them sleeping while the others picked. Seventy-two hours later it was all done, and mountains of apples rose from the wooden bins in the sales shed: Golden Delicious, Winesap, Arkansas Black.

Happily exhausted, the tenants were standing there admiring the fruits of their labor when they heard gravel crunching under tires behind them and turned around to see a sixteen-wheeler with Florida plates backing into the shed. Two big guys with bulging biceps got out and started loading apples into the truck without even introducing themselves first, and when one of the tenants went up to negotiate the ten percent business, one of the big guys just picked him up and set him out of the way.

So the rest of the tenants held a quick huddle and decided to introduce the truckers to the mountain version of People's Court. One of them cranked up the Bobcat while the others got hold of some pitchforks and pruning hooks and before long they had persuaded the landowner's men to return to Florida empty-handed. "Get lost," they explained, and the big guys did just that.

And you know the tenants were wrong. It was not their orchard. They had made a deal. The vineyard owner also deserved his share of the produce, but there is something about that story that just does not sit right. Maybe it is the casual mention of slavery that seems to be taken for granted, or maybe it is because no one likes an absentee landlord. Or maybe it is because some of us had parents or grandparents who were sharecroppers and we know how hard that life can be: tending someone else's land, bringing in someone else's harvest, making someone else's profit.

It is not the American way. From the very beginning, this country has fueled the dreams of disenfranchised people from all over the world who have come here looking for their own small piece of paradise. Some of my ancestors were Irish tenant farmers who left their homes in County Monahan to come here seeking land grants. They sailed across the ocean to start a new life in the new world farming land of their own and they worked until they made their dream come true.

That is the American way: to own your own home on your own land and preferably to grow your own vegetables for your own supper table. None of this always-looking-over-your-shoulder-handing-your-profit-over-to-someone-else stuff. Most of us in this country believe in ownership, autonomy, and self-reliance. Whether or not we can pull them off, those are the values we have been taught and those are the values we strive to live by.

If Jesus' parable is to be believed, however, those are not the values of the kingdom. Ownership of the vineyard is not the issue. It is not for sale and never will be. The owner is not looking for buyers; he is looking for tenants who will give him his share of the produce at harvest time, which means that the real issue is stewardship—a word that puts most of us on the defensive because it challenges our sense of ownership.

We have worked hard for what we have, whether it is a hundred acres or a single-wide house trailer on a lot that is not much bigger. We have deeds and titles and fence lines to prove our ownership. We have registered land plats and mortgage payment books and tax bills with our names on them. We have gone to a lot of trouble to get these things and hanging on to them requires no small measure of financial courage, but according to this morning's parable we are simply deluding ourselves.

Our ancestors became divine tenants so long ago that most of us have forgotten the circumstances. Somewhere along the way someone misplaced the tenant's agreement and wrote up a deed instead. The landowner spent most of his time in another country, after all, and he was surprisingly easy to handle. When he sent messengers to remind the tenants of their agreement, all it took was a little burst of violence and those who were still alive ran away empty-handed. The owner could have sent the police, I guess, or recruited his own army of thugs. He could have returned violence for violence, but he did not. He just kept sending messengers, one after the other, each of them pleading with the tenants to come to their senses and honor their agreement with the owner of the land.

Finally, when there was a whole row of unmarked graves full of messengers outside the vineyard walls, the owner sent his son—unaccompanied and unarmed—to teach the tenants some things they had clearly forgotten. He reminded them that ownership was a game they were playing, that they were guests on the earth, not rulers, and that there was good news in that, because being guests relieved them of certain responsibilities they were not equipped to handle, like deciding who got to be rich and who got to be poor and who got to work and who did not and whose claims to full humanity should be honored and whose should be denied.

He reminded them that being guests placed them in relationship with a host who placed them into relationship with each other, and that once they got over their delusions of ownership, those relationships could be based on gratitude, not competition, so that everything necessary for life could be shared and there would no longer be too little for some because some others had too much.

He reminded them that, as guests, they had free access to far more than they could ever have earned for themselves. Instead of a vineyard full of one-acre tracts divided by barbed wire, they had acres and acres at their disposal—not to own but to use and enjoy—through the generosity of the owner. All he asked was that they take care of it and that they give him a portion of what they produced, not because he needed it—he turned right around and gave it away himself, after all—but because *they* needed it. They needed to give in order to remember who they were: grateful guests, who took their lives into their hands like wrapped and ribboned gifts and who returned the favor by giving themselves away to others.

The tenants killed the son too, but he would not stay dead and to this day he is still haunting the vineyard, reminding us that we are God's guests—welcome on this earth and welcome to it so long as we remember whose it is and how it is to be used. We can love it as our own. We can water it by hand and build fires against the frost and take deep pleasure in the harvest. We can even will pieces of it to our children, naming them our successors in the stewardship of the vineyard.

All we may not do is spurn the owner and persecute his messengers, because to do that is to court our own destruction. To do that is to forget who we are and where we came from. We are God's sharecroppers. We tend the earth and its riches on someone else's behalf. We are expected to represent God's interests, being as generous with each other as God is with us. We are not owners. We were never meant to be. It is not the American way, but it is the kingdom way, and I will tell you something: the harvest will take your breath away.

Dreaming the Truth

Jacob left Beer-sheba and went toward Haran. He came to a certain place and stayed there for the night, because the sun had set. Taking one of the stones of the place, he put it under his head and lay down in that place. And he dreamed that there was a ladder set up on the earth, the top of it reaching to heaven; and the angels of God were ascending and descending on it. (Genesis 28:10-12)

ONE THING IS certain: Jacob does not deserve the dream he dreams. He is a two-time double crosser, who has robbed his brother of his birthright and his blessing. He is an accomplished deceiver, who has pulled the wool over his own smooth hands and his father's blind eyes in order to steal what he wants. He is a con man on the run, who owes his compromised life to his conniving mother's love.

"I am weary of my life because of the Hittite women," she complains to his father Isaac, inventing a reason for Jacob to leave town before his brother Esau can kill him, and on that pretense he goes, setting off for his uncle Laban's house in search of a more suitable wife. He goes alone, apparently, and he goes on foot, heading into the hill country with no more than he can carry—no tent, no torch, no donkey for company. He walks north on a high ridge, with the sun warming his face until it goes down. Then dusk gives way to dark and he can no longer see to walk. All he can see, on the high path ahead of him, is a flat place—"a certain place"—set about with stones. Choosing one for a windbreak and another for a pillow, he lies down in that place, where he falls into exhausted sleep, the kind of sleep in which you sink through darkness for a long, long time before coming to rest someplace very deep and very, very still.

It is in that place that the dream begins, the dream of a ladder with its bottom step on earth, leading up and out of sight with the whole company of heaven passing to and fro upon it. If the Dream-Giver makes mistakes, this looks like one. There must be a hundred people back in the promised land who have prayed for a dream like this, people who have kept their vows and done their duties, dedicating themselves to the service of God. Jacob is not one of them. He is on no vision quest; he has simply pushed his luck too far and has left town in a hurry. He is between times and places, in a limbo of his own making. The promised land is a memory; Haran is no more than a name on a map. Jacob is nowhere, which is where the dream touches down—not where it should be but where he is.

No sooner does he behold the vision than he discovers the Lord beholding it too, standing beside him making promises—nine of them in all: "I am with you...I will give you...I will not leave you...I have promised you." It is so much more than is called for. A simple word of encouragement would have done, something like, "I am keeping an eye on you, son. Clean up your act in Haran, okay?" But no. God holds nothing back, tucking everything but money into the pocket of this thief.

When Jacob wakes, he is still a double-crosser and a deceiver, but he is also God's chosen one, a visionary who does not mistake what he has seen. "How awesome is this place!" he declares to the high, thin air. "This is none other than the house of God, and this is the gate of heaven." He does not deserve the dream but he needs it, and what is more, he believes it. When he awakes, he does not write the whole thing off to anxiety or indigestion. He accepts it as God's gift to him—a true thing that happened to him in a reality lodged somewhere between this world and another, a true vision of the ladder connecting the two in the middle of nowhere.

The same kind of thing had happened to his grandfather, years and years ago—before the angels came, before his father was born, before the awful time on the mountain with the fire, the knife and, praise God, the ram. Before any of that had come to pass, Abraham had cut his covenant with God in the dark belly of a deep sleep, where the vision of a smoking fire pot and a flaming torch changed his life and the lives of his descendants forever.

The dream formed them. It plucked them from obscurity and made them a people of the dream, in which the Lord became their Lord and set them apart to bless all the families of the earth. The dream formed them and made them dreamers, too—first Abraham with his fire pot, then Jacob with his ladder, then Joseph with his sheaves of dreams, all of them true, all of them sent by God to guide God's people, from grandfather Abraham to Joseph, ruler of Egypt, to Joseph, husband of Mary, who dreamed his holy family to safety in Egypt and dreamed them back home again.

What each of them discovered was what Jacob discovered that night sleeping among the stones: that there is a busy path between heaven and earth, with the messengers of God scurrying back and forth upon it. The good news they bear is the news on Jacob's lips when he woke up: "Surely God is in this place—and I did not know it!" What had looked to him like no place turned out to be God's place. What had looked to him like an ordinary pile of rocks turned out to be the gate of heaven, and he set his stone pillow up as a pillar to mark the spot. Bethel, he called it, pouring oil on the rock: House of God.

Do you know where your Bethel is? The place where the dream of God was so real to you that you can still remember how the air smelled, how the light fell, how your heart beat so hard you thought it might break? If you do know, then treasure that knowledge always and go back there as often as you can. But if you do not know—because you have not found it yet or you cannot find your way back—well, do not be too hard on yourself. You have got a lot of company.

We dreamers are not what we used to be. We do not have time to dream, for one thing. We are too busy leading, managing, ministering, feeding, teaching, fixing, pleasing, working to dream. In order to dream, you must be able to flee all that and lie down in a lonely place now and then, a place where there is nothing going on but the slow passage of stars across the sky and a slight wind with a whisper in it. You must be willing to waste time, lie low, be good for nothing for a while.

That is another problem, I think—being good. Jacob was not, particularly, but God did not seem to mind that. Jacob was *alive*, and that was what God required. Last fall I corresponded briefly with an old man I met in upstate New York. He was a great golfer in his day. Now he walks the links at dawn when he cannot sleep, exploring the roughs and woods along the manicured fairways. It has taught him something, he says. "If you always hit the ball straight, you miss a lot of the territory." What dreams have we missed in the rough, I wonder, because we have worked so hard to stay on the green?

We are too busy to dream; we may even be too good to dream, but it is more than that. We have also lost confidence in our dreams, or perhaps I should say *our* dream, because it belongs to all of us and not to any one of us alone: the dream of a healed earth full of holy people, where we see no longer in a mirror dimly but face-to-face at last. It is a dream of reunion, of divine communion, the kind of dream in which you seem to have stumbled upon your true home and want never to leave it, a dream in which the presence of God is as real and reassuring as a hand on your shoulder or a voice in your ear. It is a dream where you would stay forever if you could, but you cannot. Sooner or later you must wake up, opening your eyes on a world so different from the dream that you almost wish you did not dream at all, but that is not a choice. You are a dreamer. That is who you are. Your only choice is what to do with your dreams: tell them or keep them to yourself? Believe them or dismiss them as your own inventions?

We are all dreamers, but dreamers have fallen upon hard times. For Jacob and his kin, a dream was a doorway into another reality—a spiritual dimension in which God spoke to men and women at the deepest levels of their beings, using the symbolic language of the dream to tell them what they needed to know. It was as natural a way for God to act as any other way, for people whose sense of reality was wide open and full of wonder. The problem is that ours is not, anymore. We belong to a people whose sense of reality is much more limited. We have been schooled in science and philosophy; we have learned to trust what we can handle and prove. We have been taught to think, not to dream, and we have lived long enough to watch many of our dreams die hard. Only saints and children still believe their dreams will come true. The rest of us are adults who know the difference between fact and fantasy. Our dreams rise to our lips and we tamp them down again, remembering how often we have been disappointed by them, reminding ourselves that there is real work to be done in the real world where dreams cannot bandage a wound or buy a loaf of bread.

So we give ourselves to that work, many of us finding real satisfaction in it. We put in long hours. We keep good records and produce measurable results: fifteen telephone calls returned, twelve more initiated; eighteen letters written for two new accounts this week; four carpools executed, six loads of laundry done, eight bags of groceries brought in under the food budget. These are facts, not fantasy. You can add them up and write them down and put them under your pillow at night when you limp home from another twelve-hour day and fall exhausted into your bed, a refugee of your own wrecked economy.

But do not be surprised if the ragged curtains of your sleep are drawn aside some dark night, and a warm breath makes the hairs on the back of your neck stand up, and the sound of high, tinkling voices fills your ears, and you begin to see something where there was nothing just a moment before: first the light, then the shape, then the dawning of

the dream in full color—not your dream but God's dream—
more vivid than life, showing you what no one could ever
have told you to your face, revealing to you what you would
never have believed. Look but also listen; strain to hear the
words that go with the pictures, the voice that is always
calling you, saying, "I am with you...I will give you...I will
not leave you...I have promised you." Look and listen well,
because this is the voice that tells the truth. This is the vision that reveals the promise. This is the dream that
changes the future by remembering the past, giving shape to
life, giving meaning and daring and hope. We may not deserve it, but we need it, and we need above all to believe
that it is true.

We are the dreamers of the promise, set apart to bless all
the families of the earth. It is not something we do with a
lot of grandeur, because of how the dream comes to us. It
comes when we have run out of the things we can get for
ourselves. It comes when all our conniving has blown up in
our faces and our luck has run out. There, in the middle of
nowhere, is where the dream touches down, reminding us
that we sleep at the gate of heaven, where it has pleased
God to be with us.

When we wake, it is our privilege to declare to all who
will listen that they sleep there too, where the bright rungs
of God's ladder touch down on our own ordinary pieces of
the earth. It is our happy calling to describe the dream in
great detail, inviting others to dream it with us, and setting
up pillars to mark all the spots where it is coming true—not
just one of them and not just two, but a forest of pillars so
thick you cannot move without bumping into one—so that
all who see them know that Bethel is not somewhere but
everywhere in this wide world that the good Lord has consented to call home.

Striving with God

The same night Jacob got up and took his two wives, his two maids, and his eleven children, and crossed the ford of the Jabbok. He took them and sent them across the stream, and likewise everything that he had. Jacob was left alone; and a man wrestled with him until daybreak. (Genesis 32:22-24)

WHEN I WORRY about the future of the church, one of the things I worry about is that there is not more wrestling in the pulpit. It is not the preacher's own struggle to proclaim the word that I miss. There is plenty of that. It is the apparent tameness of the word itself, as if our relationship with God were settled and all the rules were clear: be a good person and God will be good to you; flee bad company and rise above adversity; if you have wild dreams in the middle of the night, please keep them to yourself.

This may not be what is preached, but it is often what is heard, if only because humankind has such a high need to control the chaos of life on earth. You do not hear much about God causing the chaos, or even having a role in it. On the contrary, it is God's job to make it stop. God is supposed to restore the status quo and help everyone feel comfortable again. Isn't that how you know when God is present? When the danger has been avoided? When your heart stops pounding and you can breathe normally again? You know that God is there when you are not afraid anymore and you can feel your strength coming back like blood rushing into a numb limb.

It is an appealing idea, but unfortunately the Bible will not back it up. In that richly troubling book, much of God's best work takes place in total chaos, with people scared half

107

out of their wits: Elijah, trembling under his broom tree, pleading with God to take his life; Mary, listening to an angel's ambitious plans for plunging her into scandal; Paul, lying flat on his belly on the Damascus Road with all his lights put out. Perhaps because we know how these stories turn out, we overlook the wrestling—the stark terror of being jumped on by an unknown assailant, the collapse of the known world, the reduction of everything one has been and done to this scorched moment of fighting for one's life.

It is not the experience of God most believers seek. In his Christmas oratorio, "For the Time Being," W. H. Auden sums up "the wild prayer of longing" that rises from the average human household:

> O God, put away justice and truth for we cannot understand them and do not want them. Eternity would bore us dreadfully. Leave thy heavens and come down to our earth of waterclocks and hedges. Become our Uncle. Look after Baby, amuse Grandfather, escort Madam to the Opera, help Willy with his home-work, introduce Muriel to a handsome naval officer. Be interesting and weak like us, and we will love you as we love ourselves.

Most of us have learned to choose our words more carefully than that, but the longing is the same: for protection, for prosperity, for a God who will operate within the domestic boundaries we have set for ourselves, without doing anything to frighten us unnecessarily. We want to be chosen. We want to be saved, only gently, please, by gradual degrees, so that we can see where we are going and say, "Yes, this suits me fine. I can handle this. Show me more." It is a reasonable longing. No one in his or her right mind asks to be attacked, frightened, wounded. And yet that is how it comes sometimes, the presence and blessing of God. Sometimes it comes in the middle of the night, in the desperate wrestling that is—who would have thought it?—the answer to all our prayers.

It has been twenty years since Jacob left home. Or, to be more accurate, it has been twenty years since he fled his

brother's wrath, heading into the wilderness north of Beer-
sheba where he dreamed his famous dream, proving once
and for all that God is not a moralist. Jacob is a liar and a
cheat and still he gets the dream—his own holy vision of
the traffic between heaven and earth. It should have
changed him, but it did not. Before he leaves Bethel, the
King of Deals cuts another one. Speaking to no one in particular, but loud enough for anyone at the top of the ladder
to hear, he says, "If God will be with me, and will keep me
in this way that I go, and will give me bread to eat and
clothing to wear, so that I come again to my father's house
in peace, then the Lord shall be my God, and this stone,
which I have set up for a pillar, shall be God's house." Then,
dropping his ruse, he switches his pronouns. "And of all
that you give me, I will surely give one tenth to you" (Genesis 28:20-22). All he leaves out is helping Willy with his
homework.

Jacob makes an easy target, but all of us have prayed that
Bethel prayer at one time or another, listing the several conditions for our belief in God. The first phrase is all that is
necessary. "If God will be with me...then the Lord shall be
my God." But no. We persist in telling God what it means to
be with us—to keep us safe, to feed and clothe us, to preserve our lives in peace. These are the signs we will accept.
Should God choose some other way of being with us, the
deal is off, or at least in question. There are other gods
eager to do business with us, after all, promising more for
less without all the guesswork.

A couple of weeks ago, my husband Ed and I watched the
movie *Aladdin* on videotape. We chose it as an antidote to
The Silence of the Lambs, which had made the soles of our
feet sweat, and Walt Disney was good medicine. The genie
was funny, the villain lost, and Aladdin learned the value of
being himself. There was another moral to the story, however, that was hard for a preacher to miss: namely, that a genie is much more appealing than a God. With a genie you
know that you have three wishes, which you may redeem
whenever you like. If the genie gets on your nerves in the

meantime, you can make him go back inside his lamp, where he will play solitaire until you require his services again. Your will is his command. What could be more appealing than that?

God, on the other hand, is not in the business of granting wishes. God is in the business of raising the dead, not all of whom are willing. They have perhaps witnessed the revival of a corpse. They have seen the terrible pounding on the heart, the blue lips, the shock paddles. They have smelled the fear in the air, heard the choked return of breath, like a drowned thing coming up for air. They would just as soon stay dead, at least until someone can arrange a less painful way of coming back to life. Here is how I would like it, please: a soft kiss on the lips by someone who smells of tea roses, a gentle rubbing of my hands and feet until the feeling comes back, then a warm bath, a soft robe, and a simple meal by candlelight. No talk. Just music. An oboe, if it can be arranged.

There is nothing wrong with letting God know what we want, as long as we do not mistake our list for the covenant. The covenant has no conditions. The covenant is no deal. It is God's promise to be our God, which contains within it the promise that we shall be God's people—not by our consent but by our creation. The covenant describes for us the shape of reality, which is relationship, and our only choice is whether to believe it or not. Either way we are goners, because we are not now and will never be in charge of the relationship, but if we choose to believe in it, then we may at least face into the mystery instead of away from it, and give up our illusions of control.

Have you ever noticed how we talk about that surrender? Someone says, "How are you?" and you decide to tell her the truth. "I'm crazed," you say, "my life is a mess. I hate losing control like this." Then, if she is a good friend, she laughs at you. "You don't hate losing control," she says, "you hate losing the illusion that you were ever *in* control." And she is right, but you will forget, because like almost everyone else in the world, you have been fooled into thinking that the struggle to control is what life is all about.

If it is easier to consider Jacob, consider Jacob. Twenty years ago he poached his brother's birthright and his blessing. He conspired with his mother against his father and succeeded in tearing the family apart. Then he fled with his stolen goods, picked up a dream along the way, and arrived in Haran, where he met his deal-making match in his uncle Laban. He also met the love of his life in his cousin Rachel and ended up doing fourteen years' hard labor for her hand. Domestic life was good for Jacob; there is nothing like two wives, two mistresses, and eleven children to snuff the illusion of control. But Jacob's deal-making days were not over. Laban owed him one and Jacob collected, building up flocks as spotted and speckled as his own soul. Then it was time to go home. "Return to the land of your ancestors and to your kindred," the Lord said to Jacob, "and I will be with you."

There it was again, that promise of relationship. So Jacob made ready to go, with no conditions this time. God had prospered him and he knew it. There were no more "ifs" in him about who his God was. "Deliver me, please, from the hand of my brother." That was all he asked, his own life and the lives of his family. He had changed, but he could not imagine that Esau had, and he feared the brother whom he had robbed not once but twice. In a late effort to repay the debt and grease his own homecoming, he sent hundreds of animals ahead of him—great flocks of sheep and goats, camels and donkeys, moving across the countryside toward Esau like the living shadows of clouds.

Then Jacob settled into a camp for the night, or at least he tried to, but a powerful restlessness had got hold of him and would not let him go. So he got up that same night and moved everyone across the river—everyone and everything—and returned to the other side alone. Of all nights to be alone! The campfire was reduced to a ring of ash and the rush of the water drowned every human sound that might have come to him from the other side. But he was not alone for long. No sooner had he caught his breath than there was someone on his back. An *ish*, the Bible says, a man, although there is some doubt about that. The Midrash calls him an angel. Jacob himself says it was God who attacked him.

Whoever he is, he is strong. Jacob has lifted a stone pillar at Bethel and hauled another solid slab of rock off a well in Haran. He is a big man himself, but in this *ish*, this angel, this well-muscled God, he has found his rival. There is no talking at first, just the dull slap of flesh against flesh, as one of them gains a hold and the other one breaks it, both of them sucking air between the low grunts that seem to come from somewhere deep in the earth beneath them. That is how dark it is. They might as well be wrestling in some underground chamber for all they can see of each other, an arm snaking around the neck with no warning, a knee planted behind the blind back. They fight by feel, not by sight, until the sky lightens. Then fear gives the stranger new strength. He drops his weight and Jacob's hip cracks, but Jacob still will not turn him loose. The stranger speaks. Physical strength has failed to decide this contest; it is time to try words.

"Let me go," he says to Jacob, "for the day is breaking." According to the Midrash, he must go because he sings in the morning choir before God's throne, but Jacob is unsympathetic. He has got hold of someone who smells of heaven, and he simply will not let him go. And so Jacob, doing what Jacob does best, makes a deal. "I will not let you go," he says, "unless you bless me."

The stranger responds by asking him his name, but why? Is he getting the details he needs in order to pronounce the blessing, or is he refusing to bargain by changing the subject? "What is your name?" he asks Jacob, as they lie locked in each other's arms. If you listen hard, you can hear the echo of another question, another time when someone else who could barely see asked Jacob to identify himself. "I am Esau," he said at that time, but twenty years plus this night have changed him. "Jacob," he answers this time, and the name falls away from him like a second skin. He is no longer

112

Jacob, the supplanter. He is Israel, the survivor, the striver with God.

The stranger will not return the favor. He keeps his name to himself, but he delivers the blessing nonetheless and the nightlong embrace is over. Jacob limps toward his reunion with Esau, in whom he sees the face of God for the second time in one day. His exile is over. He is home.

When Jacob told the story later, I expect his grandchildren had a hundred questions for him.

Who was it, really?

I'm not sure.

Where did he go?

I don't know.

Will he come back?

I hope so. What am I saying? I doubt it. I don't know.

There is a question I would like to ask him. *Jacob, why didn't you run when you got the chance? When the sun came up, when he wanted you to let him go, why didn't you shout, "Glory, Hallelujah!" and head for the river?*

Because it was the most alive I had ever been in my life. Because I had never seen anything like the shining in that face and I could not bear to let it go. I thought maybe if he blessed me we would be related somehow. I thought the blessing might keep me company after he was gone.

What about your leg? Didn't it hurt?

Sure it hurt. It still hurts, but it goes with the blessing. They are a matched pair. Every time I tilt to the right and feel that hot pinch in my thigh, I remember my name. Israel. The one who strives with God.

It was the answer to his prayer at Bethel. Not the comfort and safety part, but the God-be-with-me part. It was the end of his making deals with God, the last act in his struggle to control. Jacob had learned. Not because God had nixed the deals. God had simply overlooked them, giving Jacob what he needed instead of what he wanted. God gave Jacob everything necessary for his life, which turned out to be the covenant. Within that wounded, blessed relationship, Jacob saw the face of God and lived to tell the tale. What is comfort and safety compared to that?

Of course this is all just talk until you have got a stranger on your back, smelling of heaven and pummeling you for all he is worth. When it happens, do not let anyone tell you there is something wrong. Do not let anyone convince you that if it were really God it would not be so scary and it certainly would not hurt. Hang on with everything that is in you, even if it hurts. Insist on a blessing to go with your wound and do not let go until you have got one. Then thank God for your life, limp and all, and tilt your way home.

Listening to Your Life

But Joseph said to his brothers, "Do not be afraid! Am I in the place of God? Even though you intended to do harm to me, God intended it for good, in order to preserve a numerous people, as he is doing today. So have no fear; I myself will provide for you and your little ones." (Genesis 50:19-21)

THE STORY OF Joseph and his brothers may be the most satisfying tale in all of Hebrew scripture. With a plot worthy of Shakespeare, it has everything in it: passion, foreign intrigue, reversal, revenge. Throughout it all, Joseph blossoms like some ancient Cinderella. Sold into slavery by his jealous half-brothers, he winds up ruler of Egypt, so changed that they do not even recognize him when they show up, years later, to beg him for food. He could have gotten even with them then, but he did not. Well, he got even a little. He tortured them a little, taking one of the brothers hostage and framing another as a thief. But in the end he revealed himself to them and took them into his household, where he cared for them until his death. Doing so, he brought the book of Genesis to a happy end. The saga that began with banishment from the garden of Eden and violence between earth's first two brothers ends with a family reunion in a land of plenty.

The only character missing from Joseph's story is God. Earlier in the book of Genesis, God was never hard to find. In the beginning, the Creator was there every day, tending the garden and talking with the two who lived there. When they left, God followed them into the world beyond Eden, speaking directly to their descendants. Noah, Abraham, Isaac, and Jacob—they all heard the voice of God telling them they were on the right track, telling them what to do. All that changed with Joseph. By the time he arrived on the scene, God had become silent. Not absent, just silent. There were no more divine speeches, no clear sets of instructions or otherwise audible proofs of God's presence.

When Joseph wanted to hear the voice of God, he listened to his life—to his dreams, to the people he met along the way, to the things that happened to him each day. These were how God spoke to him and he learned to be a good interpreter of them, paying close attention to all the events of his life, even the ones that hurt and frightened him, the ones that seemed to go against the will of God. They may not have made sense to him one by one, but by the time his brothers showed up he could see the pattern. No one explained it to him, but he could see God's fingerprints all over the place.

The brothers themselves were no help at all. Although Joseph had already forgiven them for what they had done to him, they were still afraid of him. Maybe it was his strange Egyptian hairdo or the accent he had picked up down south, but I do not think so. I think it was their own guilt that kept them afraid of their brother. They knew they had wished him dead. Ten against one, they had thrown him into a pit to die. Ten against one, they had changed their minds, deciding to sell him for a profit rather than kill him for free. Ten against one, they had dipped his robe in the blood of a dead goat and taken the gruesome thing back to their father. All of that, and now he was saving their lives.

It would have been easier for them if he had beaten them first, or had made them his slaves for the rest of their lives. They might have understood that better, because that is how the world works. Crime and punishment. Retaliation and revenge. But Joseph did not see it that way. He was nobody's victim. When he looked at his life, he did not see a series of senseless tragedies. He saw a lighted path. Part of it led through a pit in the ground, then down to Egypt with his hands tied behind his back. At one point it wound for years through Pharaoh's prison, but when he looked down at his feet, there it was—the road that had led him straight to where he stood.

"It was not you who sent me here but God," Joseph reassured his brothers when he first told them who he was. "Do not be distressed or angry with yourselves because you sold me here; for God sent me before you to preserve life." Then he told them to go fetch their father Jacob and to come live with him, because that was the only way the spell of guilt would ever be broken—not by the ones who had done the wrong but by the one who had suffered it. Joseph was the one with the power to set things right and he did, by reinterpreting what had happened between them and removing the blame.

His brothers did not get it, then or ever. They operated under a different understanding of cause and effect, but Joseph's offer was the difference between life and death for them, so they went and brought Jacob back to Egypt. Their brother remained a mystery to them. They never really trusted him, and when their father died they were back at it again—ten against one—scheming to save their lives. Which were not in any danger, by the way, but try telling that to a clutch of guilty people. They are so stuck in their own wrongdoing that they think everyone else is up to the same thing.

So they went to their brother Joseph, mentioning a little something he may have missed during the vigil around Jacob's bed. "Your father gave this instruction before he died," they said, delivering it verbatim: "'Say to Joseph: I beg you, forgive the crime of your brothers and the wrong they did in harming you.'" It may or may not have been true, but that was beside the point. According to the rabbis, one may lie if it is on behalf of peace. It was also beside the point because for Joseph nothing was beyond the creative power of God—not lies, not treachery, not years in prison, not death.

The things that happened to Joseph were not trivial. They mattered a great deal, and if you read the last several chapters of Genesis you will find that Joseph weeps his way through them. But all of those things were redeemable, depending on how they were used. By themselves they had no meaning. Their meaning was what God and Joseph made of them. "You meant evil against me," Joseph said to his brothers, "but God meant it for good."

He was not blaming them. He was just explaining reality to them, which they had misunderstood up to that point. They had thought *they* were in charge of the meaning of things—that the goodness or badness of an event was dependent on the human intent in it. That is why they were still so guilty. If they meant evil when they sold their brother into slavery, then evil it was for them. Even if they were sorry afterwards, so sorry they could not stand their own company, there was no going back for them. The cement of their history had hardened around their ankles and they were stuck with who they were.

What they had not reckoned on was the intent of God, which is far more inventive. God is like one of those genius sculptors who can make art out of anything. Give him a tire rim, a wrecked bicycle, a brass bedpost, and some old duct work and he will weld it all into an eagle. Nothing is too bent to be used—not even tragedies, not even bad decisions, not even plain human meanness. "You meant evil against me," said Joseph, who was a living work of art, "but God meant it for good." It not only sums up his story. It also sums up the entire human story to that point—the snake, the forbidden fruit, the murdered brother, and all the rest of it. "You meant it for evil, but God meant it for good."

It is a statement about divine providence, and we have all heard the variations on it. "God will find a way." "The Lord will provide." "God won't give you more than you can bear." "Whatever God asks of you, God will also give you what it takes to do it." Platitudes like that have always irritated me. I know they are true. That is not the problem. The problem is how they are so often said, by people with big liquid eyes who smile knowingly and pat you on the arm. I know they mean well, but I rarely feel comforted by their assurances. More often I feel dismissed. "There, there, dear, I know you're hurting, but I don't really want to hear about it. The Lord will provide. Run along now, and say your prayers."

In his brilliant book on Genesis, Walter Brueggemann talks about the tension built into the story of Joseph and his brothers. There are two very real dimensions to it, he says. First, real human jeopardy. Real betrayal. Real grief. Real famine. Real weeping. And second, real divine faithfulness. Real rescue. Real blessing. Real healing. Real food. Each reality depends on the other, he says. Elevate one at the expense of the other and you blow the whole equation, because neither one is the truth all by itself.

All by itself, the human situation looks pretty bleak. We do terrible things to each other. Our fear and our greed make monsters out of us. Nations that are not at war with other nations are at war within themselves, and the battle goes on inside each one of us. We really are in great jeopardy, and if that is all we know then we are doomed to despair, because there is no way out for us, not under our own steam. But jumping from that to absolute certainty about God's plan is not the answer, not all by itself. Because all by itself, that conviction ignores human suffering. It turns into a kind of religious romanticism that sees only what it wants to see and discounts the rest of human experience. Mortal pain and doubt have no place in this scheme, except as failures of faith. All that counts is the coming victory. Everything else is illusion. Can you imagine someone leaning down over the edge of the pit while the brothers are busy bargaining with the slave traders and yelling, "Don't worry, Joseph, everything will turn out just fine in the end"?

It would be a miserable denial of God—the God who does not live way up above us somewhere, pulling the strings and calling the shots, but the God who lives right here in the midst of us, giving us our freedom and holding the divine breath while we make our choices. Sometimes they are very good and sometimes they are very bad. Either way, God does not leave. God is committed to us and to working through us, which is what divine providence is all about. Contrary to what most of us have been taught, it is not about God's will overriding our own. It is more like a dance, that totally mysterious dance that takes place between God's freedom and our freedom, between God's will and our own. In this dance, it is not God's job to keep bad things from happening. They do happen. Brothers turn against brothers. People are bought and sold. Famine devastates the land. God's job is not to prevent these things from happening. God's job is to stay present in them and to keep on being God, creating whole worlds out of total chaos, breathing life into piles of dust, taking the unfathomable wreckage of our lives and making something fine out of them in spite of us. Because that is who God is.

Sometimes it is obvious and sometimes it is not. Sometimes the work of God's hand is so evident that you can see it a mile away and sometimes you have to dust for fingerprints. Sometimes the voice seems to come straight from heaven and sometimes it comes through the voices of strangers and friends. When Joseph wanted to hear God, he listened to his life—all of it—and what he learned he told his brothers before he died. "God will visit you," he told them. And he was right.

Judgment

Choose This Day

*I call heaven and earth to witness against you today that I have
set before you life and death, blessings and curses. Choose life so
that you and your descendants may live, loving the LORD your
God, obeying him, and holding fast to him; for that means life to
you and length of days, so that you may live in the land that the
LORD swore to give to your ancestors, to Abraham, to Isaac,
and to Jacob. (Deuteronomy 30:19-20)*

FOR YEARS NOW, I have spent my vacations walking. Every
winter a company in California sends me a fat catalog of
trips that lead in and out of some of the most rugged country in the world. All I have to do is pick one, get in shape,
and show up. The trip leader does the rest and I am always
eager to meet that person, because for ten days or two
weeks, he will tell me when to wake up, where to go, when
to stop, and what to eat.

I always watch the trip leader's face very carefully as the
group assembles at the airport, because he has never laid
eyes on any of us before and yet it is his job to get us from
point A to point B—usually eight or ten miles a day, over
two or three mountains—come rain, snow, or blisters. You
can almost see him wince when someone gets off the airplane wearing brand new everything—a sure clue that she
has never walked with a pack before—or when someone
shows up twenty pounds overweight and gets winded from
riding the airport escalator.

It is all moot at that point. The trip leader is stuck with
us and the only question is how clever he will be at getting
us to move along, especially when we are tired, hungry, wet,
or homesick. Sometimes, when you have walked six hours

in steady rain and your boots gush muddy water every time you take a step and all you have to look forward to is a long night in a wet sleeping bag, it is hard to remember that this is something you wanted to do. You start daydreaming about all the comfortable things you left behind—your car, your bed, your closet full of dry clothes; you start thinking maybe next year you will rent a condominium at the beach. And that is when the trip leader earns his pay.

"What an adventure!" he says. "Think what a great story this will make. Cheer up! It could be worse! You could be bored! Is anybody bored?"

I tell you all this because it is as close as I will ever get to understanding what went on between Moses and the chosen people in the wilderness. A two-week trek is not a forty-year exodus, but Moses was a trip leader all the same, with the orneriest bunch of walkers anyone ever had to move from point A to point B. They whined and balked and criticized his leadership. They demanded better food, more water, a shorter route, and they got all nostalgic about the good old days in Egypt when they were well-fed slaves.

In the thirtieth chapter of the book of Deuteronomy, Moses is almost done with them. Their long trek is almost over. The promised land is on the horizon and he knows that he will not be going there with them. This is his farewell speech to them, as he looks at the folks who started out with brand new everything and whose torn packs are now hanging by one knotted strap. He looks at the once overweight ones whose baggy pants are held up now with bits of twine, and he lets them know that the time has come for them to choose.

He will not be making decisions for them anymore. He has gotten them to their destination. He has taught them everything he knows and now it is their turn to choose: life or death, prosperity or adversity. Reviewing God's covenant with them, Moses reminds them what it takes to live: love God, walk in his ways, observe the commandments. In the same way, he refreshes their memory about what will kill them: turn away from God, do not listen, bow down to other gods and serve them.

These are not threats, mind you. They are simply statements of fact. Walk out a second-story window and you will fall. Hold your breath long enough and you will pass out. Turn away from God and you will perish, because only God has the power to sustain life. The chosen people knew that, but they forgot a lot. Or, more accurately, they kept hoping it was not so, because if only God had the keys to life then that left them sort of, well, dependent on him, and God's idea of a good time was not always their idea of a good time.

Manna, for instance. Granted, it was ingenious to make the stuff fall from the sky like cereal snowflakes, and the taste was all right, although a little too sweet, but the problem was the lack of variety. It was manna on Monday, manna on Tuesday, manna on Wednesday. How about a nice Greek salad on Thursday, or a kosher sausage on Friday? But no. God's menu was manna and manna it was.

Water was another problem. You would have thought that if the Lord God was going to move six hundred thousand people through the wilderness, he would have chosen a route with some watering holes on it. But no, they went thirsty until their heads were pounding and none of the children could walk anymore. Then they had to threaten Moses—not once, but twice—until he banged a rock with his stick and water came out. Can you believe that? A simple oasis with a few trees would have been a lot easier and much more comfortable.

Finally, there was Moses himself. A very stern guy, as trip leaders went—entirely humorless, pious beyond words. They were grateful to him, make no mistake, but his expectations of them were too high. He expected them to be as single-minded as he was, to walk and walk and walk without complaint, to believe that God was guiding them on their tortuous path. That was all right for him, maybe, but they were just ordinary human beings. They needed a break, some way to unwind.

So when Moses went up Mount Sinai and did not come back down for weeks and weeks, they got creative. They collected all their gold jewelry, melted it down, and made a little golden calf to worship. They thought they might have better luck getting what they wanted from a small, portable god—something they could carry around with them, something they had made all by themselves. The God who had made them turned out to be too hard to deal with, so they switched over to a god they had made instead.

It should have killed them, only Moses intervened. He ground the calf to gold dust and soon they were on their way to the promised land again. But it was a remission and not a cure, and to this day the people of God show a marked weakness for golden calves. Our reasons have not changed all that much through the years. The God who made us is still hard to deal with, God's ways are still not our ways, and our comfort still does not seem to be very high on his list of priorities.

So we are always fooling around in our spiritual basements, cooking up alternative gods that promise to be more responsive to our needs. If you think you do not have any, I can suggest several golden calf detectors. Your checkbook, for instance. What is it you invest in most heavily? What do your check stubs teach you about what you worship? Or your calendar. What gets the lion's share of your time— which, after all, is more precious than your money? When it comes time to rest, or pray, or wait on the Lord, what gets in the way? Whatever it is, it is a golden calf for sure. A job that promises security. A house that promises comfort. A portfolio that promises protection. A relationship that promises safety. A position in the community that promises power. A car that promises prestige. All the little golden calves lined up on our mantelpieces—none of them bad things, by the way, did you notice?

The raw material of a golden calf is almost never a bad thing. It is usually a good thing—like gold—made into an ultimate thing—like God. Only that is where the trouble starts, because things are not God. They never have been, and they never will be. Things may produce results for a while; they may even produce results for a long while, but talk to someone whose job has just evaporated, or whose marriage has just ended, or whose health has just failed, and let that person tell you what a golden calf is worth. Remember that you are dust, and to dust you shall return.

God, on the other hand—the one, true, and living God—does not seem very interested in producing results, or at least not the ones that interest us. God seems more interested in producing life—not mere pulse and respiration life, but abundant life, extravagant life, my-cup-runneth-over life, which has very little to do with comfort, security, power, or prestige.

We can bow down to those gods. That is one of our choices. We can serve them. Or we can stand up, brush the gold dust off our hands, and seek the living God—even if the food is not so good, and water is hard to come by, and the expectations are ridiculously high. It is our choice which way we will turn: toward the golden calf corral or toward the wide open spaces, the wilderness, where the true God may be found. Or, in the words of the trip leader, "I call heaven and earth to witness against you today that I have set before you life and death, blessings and curses. Choose life so that you and your descendants may live, loving the Lord your God, obeying him, and holding fast to him; for that means life to you and length of days."

That is how the passage in Deuteronomy ends. We do not know what the people answered Moses. We do not know what they chose, which leaves the question still ringing in the air for us today and every day. We have been fully informed. Heaven and earth will witness to that. The choice is ours: blessings or curses, life or death. What will it be, people of God? Let us choose this day whom we will serve.

Changed into Fire

He will baptize you with the Holy Spirit and fire. His winnowing fork is in his hand, and he will clear his threshing floor and will gather his wheat into the granary; but the chaff he will burn with unquenchable fire. (Matthew 3:11-12)

EVERY ADVENT OF our lives, we have to go by John the Baptist to get to Jesus. Drawn by the light of one particular star, we are heading through the cool blue night, minding our own quiet business, when a red glow appears just over the rise ahead. Sparks twirl up into the sky and become ash, floating away from the unseen source of heat. Reaching the top of the hill, we look down and see—you guessed it— John the Baptist, hopping mad, preaching in front of a bonfire with a pitchfork in one hand and an ax in the other.

He is the last person in the world most of us want to see. Some of us have gone to great lengths to avoid him, leaving the churches of our childhoods, switching off our radios when the gospel hour comes on, turning our heads the other way when we pass those signs along the highway that say, "Repent, for the kingdom of God is at hand." It is not a message most of us flock to hear. Over the years, John's hellfire and damnation brand of Christianity has been used to threaten us, scold us, punish us, and just plain frighten us, until few of us want anything to do with it anymore.

But there is no getting around John. He is God's appointed messenger, sent to prepare the way of the coming Lord, and his message is that the one who is coming is not coming to host a tea party. He is coming to chop and to burn. He is coming to cut a narrow swath through the world, separating the trees that bear good fruit from those that are dead wood and winnowing the life-sustaining wheat from the worthless chaff.

He is coming to judge the world, in other words. He is coming to determine who is on the side of life and who is not, and to dispatch those who are not so that he and the good fruit, the good wheat, can get on with the business of feeding a starving world. It is not that he hates the dead wood or the chaff; it is not that he is out to get them. There is simply no life left in them for the Lord of life to reach, and meanwhile they are in the way. So he will cut and sweep and burn, John says, as part of his coming to the world. He will judge between those who are on the way and those who are in the way as he clears his own way through the world, and all of us shall know ourselves for who we are.

I do not know anyone who looks forward to judgment, do you? I see this awful image of a heavenly line-up, where all of us are standing backed up against a white wall with bright lights in our eyes and numbers around our necks, facing a two-way mirror behind which we know the Lord himself is looking us over, determining whether we are on his team or not. "Numbers 2, 5, 8, 9, and 12—dismissed!" the voice over the loudspeaker says. I look down and see the nine around my neck. I have been found out. A door opens at the end of the corridor and I shuffle out behind the others, into a place of intense heat and licking flames.

One of the most frightening things about John's vision of judgment is that unquenchable fire of his. It is not possible to live in the Bible belt without a vivid image of hell, much more vivid than the clean streets of heaven. But if you read the Bible very much, you have to wonder about that fire. Throughout holy scripture, fire is the one reliable sign of the presence of God. God speaks to Moses out of the burning bush; a pillar of fire guides the people of Israel through the wilderness after their escape from Egypt; when Moses goes up on Mount Sinai to get the ten commandments from God, it looks to those down below as if the mountain itself is being devoured by fire.

I do not mean to minimize the danger. This is not safe fire; it can still burn and kill. But it is God's own fire, the fire of God's presence, fire that wants to speak to us, guide us, instruct us, save us. It is the fire of a potter who wants to make useful vessels out of damp clay. It is the fire of a jeweler who wants to refine pure gold from rough ore. It does not have to be the fire of destruction, in other words. It may also be the fire of transformation, a fire that both lights us up and changes us, melting us down and reforming us more nearly to the image of God. It is the fire with which Jesus himself baptizes us, inviting us into bright, hot relationship with him. Even when the fire seems bent on consuming us, like Meshach, Shadrach, and Abednego in the fiery furnace we find that we have company, and that even in the hottest regions of our own personal hells we do not sweat alone.

Judgment is above all about being known like that, all the way down. It is about being seen through, seen into, and known for who we really are. It is about the total failure of our defenses and the abject poverty of our pretensions. It is about stepping into the light, or having the light turned upon us, so that every nook and cranny of our being is illuminated for examination. It is about standing before God without our armor, our masks, our possessions, our excuses, with nothing but our beating hearts and the slim volume of our life histories to commend us, waiting to hear God's true word about ourselves.

And oh, how we want it. And oh, how we fear it. We want so much to be known—really known—and to have the truth about ourselves told. And we fear so much being known—really known—and having the truth about ourselves told. Maybe the only people who look forward to judgment are those who have no doubts about their own goodness. I could not say; I do not know any of them.

Still, it seems vitally important to remember that our salvation depends, finally, not on our own goodness but on the goodness of the judge, who is not some stranger behind a glass wall but a savior—a saver of life—who has pledged us his presence, his help, and his love. John did not know that part yet. He had not yet met the Lord whose way he was preparing, and once he had met him, he had doubts about him, because the Messiah turned out to be so much gentler than John had expected, so much more willing to forgive.

Jesus is the judge, yes, but his chambers are the chambers of his compassionate heart. No judgment takes place outside of there; all judgment takes place inside there, by the same Lord who offers us peace, pardon, and transformation every day of our lives. We can refuse him, of course. We can fail to believe him, we can fear him, we can run away from him. Or we can say yes, here I am, see me the way I really am, tell me the whole truth about myself, refine me, transform me, baptize me with the Holy Spirit and with fire and damn the torpedoes. I give up trying to figure out how good or bad I am. I give up trying to be God. You be the judge. You be God. You have better credentials anyway.

One thing you can say for sure about judgment is that it will have far less to do with who we are than with who God is. And if we can face the prospect of it with our eyes wide open, it is not because we are confident in our own goodness but because we are confident in God's goodness, and confident above all in the fiery, transforming power of God to create sons and daughters of Abraham out of stones, or out of any one of us, for that matter. God does not need much in the way of raw materials—not a chest full of merit badges or an unsullied reputation or even a clean conscience. All God needs to create a human being is a handful of dust willing to be transformed, willing to be caught on fire for heaven's sake.

There is an old story about a saint named Abbot Joseph, one of the spiritual masters of the fourth century who were known as the desert fathers. Abbot Joseph was in charge of a large community of monks living in the desert, and his main job was to instruct the young monks who came to him for spiritual guidance. One day one of those monks came to see him, clearly forlorn. He had followed all the rules, done everything right, but still he felt there were something missing. "Father," he said to Abbot Joseph, "according as I am able, I keep my little rule, and my little fast, my prayer, meditation, and contemplative silence; and according as I am able I strive to cleanse my heart of thoughts. Now what more should I do?" Abbot Joseph rose up in reply and stretched out his hands to heaven, and his fingers became like ten lamps of fire. He said, "Why not be totally changed into fire?"

With Power and Great Glory

But in those days, after that suffering, the sun will be darkened, and the moon will not give its light, and the stars will be falling from heaven, and the powers in the heavens will be shaken. Then you will see "the Son of Man coming in clouds" with great power and glory. (Mark 13:24-26)

TWO WEEKS AGO I went to see my friend John Hobbs at Nacoochee Presbyterian Church. He showed me through the new fellowship hall that is under construction there and then we went into the church, where a curious thing sat on the communion table. It was a fat white candle sitting in a deep dish with a spiral of rusted barbed wire climbing the air around it. "What is *that?*" I asked him, thinking it had something to do with the church's prison ministry. "It's a symbol I came across that really spoke to me," he said, gently touching one of the steel barbs. "See, the light has already come into the world, but there is still work to be done. There is still darkness between us and the light."

There is not any barbed wire around the candles we put on our Advent wreath, but in their own way they remind us of the same thing. There are four of them, one for each Sunday before Christmas. With one candle lit they tell us when our new year begins, and that we are on a different timetable from the rest of the world. There are plenty of other calendars that shape our lives—school calendars and fiscal calendars and national calendars, all of them with their own values and concerns. The Christian calendar focuses on the life of Christ, and what his life tells us about our own lives with God.

Perhaps you have noticed that this year of ours begins in the dark. From midsummer on the days get shorter as the earth spins away from the sun in its annual ellipse. With the end of daylight savings time in October, nighttime takes over. Then it gets dark at six o'clock and every day the dark comes sooner. By the time the earth rounds the bend on December 21, it is the shortest day of the year, barely nine hours long.

One thing Advent tells me is that people of faith know it will get darker before it gets light. That is what our calendar teaches us, beginning when it does. Week by week we will light new candles, but even as we light them the darkness will increase. We also know that the sun will come back, just like we know that God will be born in a barn in Bethlehem. These are sure facts of our lives, but so is waiting in the dark. Anyone who has ever hungered for morning knows that. It will come, but it will not be rushed. You can prop the clock right by your face on the pillow. You can count to sixty five-hundred times and it will not change a thing. Night creatures will still rustle in the leaves outside your window. Your heart will still beat like a drum in your ears. Morning will come, but it will not be rushed. Our job is to wait without losing hope.

That is what Jesus told his disciples in the thirteenth chapter of Mark. There were only four of them there to hear him—Peter, James, John, and Andrew—the inner circle, the first four to put down what they were doing and follow him. They just had walked with Jesus to the Mount of Olives and sat down with him there, looking across the Kidron Valley at the great walled city of Jerusalem, with the temple crowning it at its highest point. Jesus had told them that the whole place would come tumbling down one day soon, and they wanted him to tell them when. How would they know when the center of their universe was about to blow?

That is when he told them about the dismantling of the sky, how the stars would fall from their constellations like diamonds from a broken necklace, how the sun would be smudged and the moon snuffed out before they saw the Son of Man riding the clouds with great power and glory. He did not say it to scare them. He said it to comfort them. They needed to know that even something as frightening as the end of the world was in God's good hands. When the cosmos collapsed and every light in the sky was put out, they were to remember what he had told them. They were to remember that God is sovereign over darkness as well as light and they were to watch—watch even in the darkness—for his coming to them in the clouds.

By the time Mark wrote his words down some thirty years later, it seemed that the end was very near. The stars were still in the sky, but that was about all. The headlines were as bad then as they are now. Jerusalem lay in ruins. The temple was destroyed. The emperor's favorite pastime was thinking up inventive new ways for Christians to die and there was fighting among the Christians themselves, with whole families being torn apart by their conflicting loyalties. False messiahs were setting themselves up on every street corner, each of them claiming exclusive access to the mind of God. Everything was falling apart, and those who had believed in Jesus must have wondered if they had been fooled. Surely this was not the way things were supposed to turn out. Surely God had intended a nonviolent renovation of the world—a sort of huge urban renewal project—with loyal believers in charge. Not this chaos. Not this outrage. Not this darkness.

That is when Mark told them the story again, writing it down so they would not forget: how Jesus himself had predicted it all, how he had tried to tell them that they could not have a new world without letting go of the old one, which would have to crash and burn before anything fresh could be born in its ashes. It was and is the good news of the end of the world, a piece of the gospel most of us would just as soon forget, but there it is: when the end comes, it will not be because God is absent but because God is very present, having come in great power and glory to make all things new.

In the meantime, our job is to watch, Jesus says—not to watch out, but to watch—to stay alert, to pay attention, so that we are not snoozing when the master comes home. There are at least three different ways Christians have gone about this job in years past. For some, watching means looking for the literal end of the world. There are whole books you can buy on the mathematical formulae contained in the book of Revelation, with good advice about how to be in the right place at the right time. The only problem with this approach is that it tries to discover what even Jesus himself could not discover. "Truly," he said, "this generation will not pass away before all these things take place." And yet with his next breath he took it back. "But of that day or that hour no one knows, not even the angels in heaven, nor the Son, but only the Father." Some people say that phrase was added much later, after generations and generations of believers had passed away and those who were left wanted to know what the delay was all about, but if Jesus was fully human, it was true: even he did not know the mind of God.

Another way Christians have settled down to watch is by letting their awareness of the end heighten their commitment to the present. In colonial New England, I am told, a meeting of state legislators was plunged into darkness by a sudden eclipse, during which many of those present panicked and others moved to adjourn. But one of them said, "Mr. Speaker, if it is not the end of the world and we adjourn, we shall appear to be fools. If it is the end of the world, I should choose to be found doing my duty. I move you, sir, that candles be brought."

Yet a third way to watch for the end is to suspect that there is not just one end to the world any more than there is just one coming of Christ to look forward to. When Jesus died, his disciples believed the world had ended. When Jerusalem fell and Nero swooped down on the young church like a mad vulture, they believed the world had ended. In a manner of speaking, the world can end any day of the week with a declaration of war, or the death of a child, or a grim diagnosis, and watching for Christ's coming again in power and great glory can become the only light in such times, when sun and moon and stars have all been snuffed out.

Whichever of these ways makes the most sense to you, they have one thing in common. The one who is coming is not an enemy but a friend. He may come in the light, but he may also come in the evening, or at midnight, or at three in the morning. Darkness does not stop him, and it does not have to stop us either. Our job is not to lie in bed with pillows over our heads or to shove all the heavy furniture in front of the door for fear of the darkness outside. Our job is to light the candle wrapped in barbed wire and set it in the window. Our job is to watch for the one who comes to us with healing in his wings and to open the door for him before he raises his hand to knock. Who knows when that will be? No one, that is who. Watch, therefore. Take heed, watch. For what he says to us he says to all: Watch.

Waiting in the Dark

There was a man sent from God, whose name was John. He came as a witness to testify to the light, so that all might believe through him. He himself was not the light, but he came to testify to the light. (John 1:6-8)

AS DIFFERENT AS the four gospels are, they all include John the Baptist. The picture we have of him comes from Matthew and Mark: a wild-eyed prophet in camel's hair and leather, with locusts and honey on his breath. The fourth gospel offers no visual effects at all. In that account, we must deduce who he is from what he says.

Who are you? *I am not the Messiah.*

Are you Elijah? *I am not.*

Are you the prophet? *No.*

Who are you? *I am the voice.*

Why are you baptizing, if you are a nobody? *There is somebody coming after me whom you do not know. The truth is, I don't know either. All I know is that I am not worthy to fiddle with his shoelaces.*

It must have been hard to be John. There he was, set apart by God to do one single thing with his life—to proclaim the coming one—and yet he did not even have a name to shout out loud. He did not know who he was waiting for nor when he was coming. He did not know whether to watch the sky or the earth. Maybe the one he was waiting for would come in a chariot of fire that no one could miss, but it was also possible that he would come incognito, so that only those who were searching for him would know he had arrived.

The net effect of all this unknowingness was that John did not know who he was himself, either. He knew what his job was, all right, but there was no name for him. The priests and Levites who came from Jerusalem tried to put a label on him. They wanted to fit him into some religious category they knew something about so that they could get a fix on him, but he utterly escaped them. How could he not? The one who was coming would defy all categories himself. He would turn the known world upside down, so what could John be but a voice crying out in the wilderness? "Make straight the way of the Lord...the one you do not know...the one who is coming after me."

Until that one came, John's life was one long Advent, a waiting in the dark for the light, a waiting without knowing for the one thing that would change everything. He could not name it, but he knew it was coming, and the knowledge alone was enough to make the wait worthwhile. On the whole, human beings are not very good at waiting. Maybe you have noticed that. We prefer to reach out and grasp what we want—either that or cross it off our lists—but the truth is that sometimes it is not there to be grasped.

Maybe it is not ripe yet, a fig that is still a hard green knot no bigger than a gumball. Or maybe it is not even real yet, a dream of the future that is still a long ways off. Waiting, we have to admit that we are not in charge here. There are things we think we cannot live without that we are denied, and there are things we had given up wanting for ourselves that are suddenly dropped in our laps. We can say yes and we can say no to these things, but we do not seem able to control them. Our lives are formed in the hands of a great mystery that does not ask us for our advice.

So if waiting is an aggravation, it is at least partly because we do not like being reminded of our limits. We like doing—earning, buying, selling, building, planting, driving, baking—making things happen, whereas waiting is essentially a matter of being—stopping, sitting, listening, looking, breathing, wondering, praying. It can feel pretty helpless to wait for someone or something that is not here yet and that will or will not arrive in its own good time, which is not the same thing as *our* own good time.

And yet waiting is an essential part of the Christian life. Listen to what we say every time we break bread together: "Christ has died. Christ is risen. Christ will come again." This is the mystery of our faith, that we are always waiting for Christ to come to us even though we believe that he has already come and that he is coming to us right now in word and sacrament. Is his coming past, present, or future? It is all three, which means that our waiting is not a matter of entering into suspended animation. Our waiting is not nothing. It is something—a very big something—because people tend to be shaped by whatever it is they are waiting for.

Have you noticed that? When you want something really badly, your whole life tends to rearrange itself around that goal. For one person it might be a baby and for someone else a house. When I was a teenager, it was independence I was waiting for—my own life by my own rules—and when I got that, it was a calling I wanted, a clear set of directions I could follow to whatever turned out to be my life. I waited years for that calling to come through and years more for a relationship with one other person that would last. I am still waiting for maturity, for enlightenment, for a bridled tongue and a contrite heart.

How about you? What are you waiting for, and how is it shaping your life? Are you waiting for certainty, for healing, for love? Are you waiting for recognition, for retirement, for enough money to pay the bills? How about peace and justice on earth, or an end to the destruction of the planet? How about the dawning of a new age, in which the wolf and the lamb shall feed together and the lion eat straw like the ox?

Whatever it is that our hearts yearn for, chances are that it has something to do with our vision of what it would mean for us to be made whole, to be transformed into people who are not afraid anymore, whose basic needs are met and whose wounds are healed and who are more nearly the people God created us to be. It is the same vision John the

Baptist had, of a great light that was coming into the world to outshine the darkness once and for all.

We may be right about what will make us whole and we may be wrong, but one big difference between us and John is that he knew he did not know. "Among you stands one whom you do not know," he told the priests and Levites who came to him, looking for handles on the mystery. Read on in the fourth gospel and you will hear him say it two more times: "I myself did not know him." John waited without knowing who he was waiting for. He waited in the dark for the light without knowing what his name was or when he would come. He understood that everything else he was waiting for boiled down to waiting for God and he was willing to forego the details, although that left him without any way to describe himself.

"Who are you?" they asked him, but he could not say.

Are you the Messiah? *No.*

Are you Elijah? *No.*

Are you the prophet? *No.*

All he could tell them about himself was that he was the voice sent to clear the way—to erase the board and wash it down—so that the unnamed, unknown, unimagined one who was coming after him would have room to work.

What are we waiting for? Let's tell the truth: we do not know, and still we are able to rejoice, because the one who is coming is the one who has come and who is coming to us even now. We may be short on details, but we are not short on hope or wonder at this mystery whose good hands we are in. Whatever happens to us while we are waiting, however dark it gets before it gets light, this is what we believe: they are *good* hands.

Transformation

Blessed are
the Upside Down

*Blessed are you when people revile you and persecute you and
utter all kinds of evil against you falsely on my account. Rejoice
and be glad, for your reward is great in heaven, for in the same
way they persecuted the prophets who were before you.*
(Matthew 5:11-12)

WHEN I WAS little, I used to like standing on my head. I was
short then. Just about everything in the world was taller
than I was, taller and very boring, but by standing on my
head I could liven things up a little. Grass hung in front of
my eyes like green fringe. Trees grew down, not up, and the
sky was a blue lawn that went on forever. For as long as I
kept my balance I could tap dance on it, while birds and
clouds flew under my feet. My swing set was no longer an
"A" but a "V" and my house seemed in danger of falling off
the yard—just shooting off into space like a rocket—leaving
a sidewalk lined with pansies that led to nowhere. I liked
standing on my head because it made me see old things in a
new way. I liked it because it made life seem exciting and
unpredictable. In a world where trees grew down and
houses might fall up, anything seemed possible.

I think Jesus should have asked the crowd to stand on
their heads when he taught them the Beatitudes, because
that was what he was doing. He was turning the known
world upside down, so that those who had been fighting for
breath at the bottom of the human heap suddenly found
themselves closest to heaven, while those who thought they

145

were on top of things found themselves flat on their backs looking up.

The formula itself was not new to anyone. Beatitudes were common expressions in those days, and not only in religious circles. They were everyday sayings about the Good Life, listing virtues that anyone would have been pleased to have. *Blessed are the wise, for they shall not be fooled. Blessed are the strong, for their enemies shall fear them. Blessed are the wealthy, for they shall never go hungry.* That sort of thing. Another word for "blessed" in this formula is "happy." The French translation is *debonair.* I like that: *Debonair are those who have invested well, for their old age shall be secure.*

What was so shocking about Jesus' list was not the form but the content. Blessed are the *meek?* The *mournful?* The *poor in spirit?* Who was he kidding? There was nothing *debonair* about any of those. What was so happy about hungering and thirsting for righteousness, or about being reviled and persecuted? "Rejoice and be glad"?! No one with a lick of sense was going to vote for any of those definitions of the Good Life, but Jesus did not ask for anyone's approval. He just redefined the Good Life in nine short sentences and held them out for everyone to see: nine portraits of kingdom people, previously known as victims, dreamers, pushovers, and fools. These are the chosen ones, he said, the blessed ones who shall see God face-to-face. These are the happy ones, the lucky ones, who shall be satisfied—not because they got an advance copy of the rules and played by them to win but because winning was the farthest thing from their minds.

This is a list of losers, make no mistake about it. The merciful who keep forgiving their enemies so their enemies can trounce them all over again. The pure in heart who believe everything they hear and empty their bank accounts to keep crooks in business. The peacemakers who step into the middle of a fist fight and get clobbered from both sides. These are God's favorites, Jesus insists—not the effective, successful people in the world but the ones who cannot even compete, who would not know success if it walked up and handed them a trophy. The blessed ones would insist there must have been some mistake. The blessed ones would give the prize away to someone who needed it more. The blessed ones would put it in a closet so they would not be tempted to think well of themselves.

Most of us do not know what to do with the Beatitudes. Some of us have heard them for so long that they have lost their shock value for us. They just sound sort of sweet and familiar to us—a Christian poem—something to needle-point and hang over the piano. Others of us hear them like new commandments and worry that we are not meek enough, pure enough, persecuted enough. But please note that there are no "shoulds" or "oughts" here, no "shalts" or "shalt nots." The language of the Beatitudes is not transactional language—do this and you will receive this; do that and you will receive that. It is descriptive language—this is who these people are now, and this is what the future holds for them. It is not the language of law but of gospel, the language of hope and promise that the way things are now is not the way they will always be, and that those who find themselves at the back of the bus now will be sitting in first class before the trip is through.

Today this same gospel is being preached around the world—in a cinder block church in Kenya, where people sit cross-legged on a packed dirt floor while carpenter bees fly in and out the open windows; in a shack on stilts in the wetlands of El Salvador, where the majority of those present must listen hard because they cannot read; or even right down the road at the Catholic church on Highway 197, where Mexicans from the trailer park have gathered to praise God in their own tongue.

Much of the power of the Beatitudes depends on where you are sitting when you hear them. They sound different from on top than they do from underneath. They sound different up front than they do in the back. Up front with the religiously satisfied and self-assured, they sound pretty confrontational. Where is your hunger and thirst, you well-fed Christians? Where is your spiritual poverty? Where are the bones of your soul showing through your clothes, and why aren't your handkerchiefs soaked with tears?

But way in the back, with the victims, the dreamers, the pushovers, and the fools, the Beatitudes sound completely different. Shhh, they say, dry your tears, little ones. The whole earth belongs to you, though someone else still holds the keys. It won't be long now. Heaven's gates are opening wide for you, and the first face you shall see shall be the face of God.

They are the same words in every place, of course. It is just the ears that change, each of us hearing Jesus' description of the Good Life through our own filters—as something foreign or something familiar; as something to be sought or something to be feared. I guess you can do anything you want to with the Beatitudes; people always have. Some have ignored them, some have admired them and walked away, some have used them as a yardstick to measure their own blessedness, and some have used them to declare revolution. The simplest thing to do with them, perhaps, is to let them stand you on your head so that you cannot see the world in the same way again, so that you cannot be sure anymore who are the winners and who are the losers.

Upside down, you begin to see God's blessed ones in places it would never have occurred to you to look. You begin to see that the poor in spirit, the meek and those who mourn are not just people you can help but people who can help you, if you will let them, and that their hunger and thirst for God are not voids to be filled but appetites to be envied.

Upside down, you begin to see that the peacemakers are not flower children but physicians, prescribing God's own tranquillity, and that the pure in heart have just never gotten the knack of locking their doors. Upside down, you begin to see that those who have been bruised for their faith are not the sad ones but the happy ones because they have found something worth being bruised for, and that those who are merciful are just handing out what they have already received in abundance.

The world looks funny upside down, but maybe that is just how it looks when you have got your feet planted in heaven. Jesus did it all the time and seemed to think we could do it too. So blessed are those who stand on their heads, for they shall see the world as God sees it. They shall also find themselves in good company, turned upside down by the only one who really knows which way is up.

Mothers of God

The virgin's name was Mary. And the angel came to her and said, "Greetings, favored one! The Lord is with you." But she was much perplexed by his words and pondered what sort of greeting this might be. (Luke 1:27-29)

WE DO NOT have stained glass windows at Grace-Calvary, but if we did, we would certainly have an annunciation window. It is one of the most beloved scenes in the whole Christian story, that intimate moment between Mary and the angel Gabriel in which everything began with a young girl's "yes" to God's proposal. Why do we love it so much? Is it the angel or Mary's courage that is so appealing? Or is it the reassurance that God can and will invade our ordinary lives, giving us our own chances to say "yes" to God's wild plans?

Throughout the centuries, artists have rendered the annunciation scene in very formal strokes, preserving Mary and the angel Gabriel for posterity in wood and paint and glass. While their styles and colors have varied, Mary is always the picture of femininity, dressed in yards and yards of silk or brocade, her golden hair plaited like a crown around her head, her nails perfectly manicured. She looks so composed that it is hard to remember she is just a girl—in her early teens, not her twenties—who has had precious little experience with men or angels or the world.

She is usually shown either spinning or reading at her prayer desk, absorbed in her work, when out of nowhere comes this magnificent angel, as beautiful as she is, dressed like a papal emissary with a tiara on his head or a garland of flowers studded with flames. In most pictures the feathers of his great, spread wings are white, but in at least one medieval painting they are the feathers of a peacock, all iridescent greens and blues. In his hand, he usually holds a lily, an olive branch, or a royal scepter—signs of the purity, peace, and authority he brings from above.

Somewhere in the annunciation scene you can usually find a dove, a sign that what is happening is under the guidance of the Holy Spirit, but down below, everything depends on Mary. Gabriel is not standing over her; he is kneeling in front of the girl upon whose answer he, and God, and the whole creation depend.

But Mary did not really get to give an answer, did she? The angel did not *ask* her if she would like to be the mother of God; he *told* her—that God had been gracious to her, that she would bear a son, and that he would be the king of Israel forever. The angel did not ask her how that sounded to her and whether she would like to try out for the role; he *told* her—the Lord is with *you*, he said—and Luke tells us that Mary was much perplexed by his words. She was a good Jewish girl, after all. She had heard about the garden of Eden and about how Eve had bungled things but good by believing what she was told by an equally strange creature. Perhaps Mary did not want to make the same mistake, so she interrogated the angel. "How can this be?" she asked him. She wanted to know exactly whose idea it was and exactly how it would happen. She wanted to make sense out of what made no sense: that God had decided to surrender himself to flesh and blood but that he needed her help, needed her surrender as well in order to make possible his own.

"How can this be?" Mary asked, and that is all she asked, but there are several other questions I believe I would have asked, such as: Will Joseph stick around? Will my parents still love me? Will my friends stand by me or will I get dragged into town and stoned for sleeping around? Will the pregnancy go all right? Will the labor be hard? Will there be someone there to help me when my time comes? Will I know what to do? You say the child will be king of Israel, but what about me? Will I survive his birth? What about me?

If any such questions occurred to Mary, she did not ask them. According to Luke, she listened as the angel told her the barest details about how it would all come to pass, and then came her turn to speak. It was *going* to happen, that much seemed clear, but still she had a choice—whether to say yes to it or no, whether to take hold of the unknown life the angel held out to her or whether to defend herself against it however she could.

Mary was the only one in the history of the world who had that particular decision to make. The eastern church knows her as *Theotokos*, "the God-bearer" who consented to carry, give birth to, nurse, and raise the son of God. Only one person was ever drafted to do that, but still it is hard to hear her story without hearing more than a little of our own. There is much talk these days about all the choices we have, and about how it is up to each one of us to choose our own lives, but more often than not they seem to choose us. Our best laid ten-year plans are interrupted by life's own plans for us: by sudden illness and surprise babies, by aging parents and the economy. Terrible things happen and wonderful things happen, but seldom do we know ahead of time exactly *what* will happen to us. Like Mary, our choices often boil down to yes or no: yes, I will live this life that is being held out to me or no, I will not; yes, I will explore this unexpected turn of events or no, I will not.

If you decide to say no, you simply drop your eyes and refuse to look up until you know the angel has left the room and you are alone again. Then you smooth your hair and go back to your spinning or your reading or whatever it is that is most familiar to you and you pretend that nothing has happened. If your life begins to change anyway, you have several options. You can be stoic. You can refuse to accept it. You can put all of your energy into ignoring it and insist in spite of all the evidence that it is not happening to you.

If that does not work, you can become angry, actively defending yourself against the unknown and spending all of your time trying to get your life back the way it used to be. And then of course you can become bitter, comparing yourself to everyone else whose lives are more agreeable than yours and lamenting your unhappy fate. If you succeed in this, your life may not be an easy one, but you can rest assured that no angels will trouble you ever again.

Or you can decide to say yes. You can decide to be a daredevil, a test pilot, a gambler. You can set your book down and listen to a strange creature's strange idea. You can decide to take part in a plan you did not choose, doing things you do not know how to do for reasons you do not entirely understand. You can take part in a thrilling and dangerous scheme with no script and no guarantees. You can agree to smuggle God into the world inside your own body.

Deciding to say yes does not mean that you are not afraid, by the way. It just means that you are not willing to let your fear stop you, that you are not willing to let your fear keep you locked in your room. So you say yes to the angel, you say, "Here I am; let it be with me according to your word," and so saying you become one of Mary's people, one more *Theotokos* who is willing to bear God into the world.

"We are all meant to be mothers of God," wrote Meister Eckhart, a medieval mystic and theologian. "What good is it to me," he continued, "if this eternal birth of the divine Son takes place unceasingly but does not take place within myself? And, what good is it to me if Mary is full of grace if I am not also full of grace? What good is it to me for the Creator to give birth to his Son if I do not also give birth to him in my time and my culture? This, then, is the fullness of time: When the Son of God is begotten in us."

Greetings, favored ones! The Lord is with you. Do not be afraid. For nothing will be impossible with God.

Believing the Impossible

Joseph, son of David, do not be afraid to take Mary as your wife, for the child conceived in her is from the Holy Spirit. She will bear a son, and you are to name him Jesus, for he will save his people from their sins. (Matthew 1:20-21)

IN LEWIS CARROLL'S children's classic, *Through the Looking Glass*, the White Queen advises Alice to practice believing six impossible things before breakfast each day. Every Christmas, Christians would do well to take the same advice. How else are we to prepare ourselves for the preposterous story we are about to hear again about how God decided to abandon heaven for earth, trading power and might for diapers and a teething ring? And how his mother could not say how it happened, exactly, although his mother's husband knew for sure that it had nothing whatsoever to do with him?

Joseph was a just man, Matthew tells us, and a kind one too. Whatever he believed about his young wife, he was not willing to shame her, either by putting her on public trial or by muddying her name to clear his own. So he resolved to divorce her quietly, without casting blame, and he was on the verge of doing so when an angel of the Lord started whispering in his ear—giving him several impossible things of his own to believe before breakfast—and nothing was ever the same again. Joseph's sense of right and wrong got lost in the divine shuffle. His righteousness gave way to God's. He believed what an angel told him in a dream, and took Mary home with him to be his wife.

But what did that make him? A father or a stepfather? A husband or a chaste roommate? The head of the household or the appointed guardian for God's own wife and child? Christian tradition has never known quite what to do with Joseph. He disappears from the gospels before Jesus is baptized and is never heard from again, which seems to support the legend that he was already an old man when he took Mary for his wife.

Study religious art and that is what you will see: a grizzled old man who has lost most of his hair, dozing off to the side somewhere with his chin on his walking stick while the whole world admires young Mary and her child. In some paintings he sits near her with his shoe off and his foot bare, snipping his long woolen stocking into a warm wrap for the child. In others, he cups a slender candle in his hand, protecting its fragile fire from the wind while his wife and child glow with celestial light. His earthbound flame is feeble against their heavenly radiance, and he seems always to be lingering just beyond the edge of the golden sphere that envelops them—the kindly old man in the dark, an extra in the drama starring Mary and her child.

He is nowhere to be seen in most renderings of the annunciation. In Luke's gospel, which is by far the most popular choice at this time of year, it is Mary and Gabriel in the stained glass window of the annunciation—Mary a tender girl dressed all in blue, clutching a white lily to her breast as the bright angel bursts in upon her, a gilded scroll issuing from his lips: "Hail, O favored one, the Lord is with you!"

But not in Matthew's gospel. In that story, it is Joseph in the window, an old man in a brown homespun robe, lying on his pallet fast asleep with his mouth slightly open as the same angel whispers in his ear: "Joseph, son of David, do not be afraid to take Mary as your wife, for the child conceived in her is from the Holy Spirit. She will bear a son, and you are to name him Jesus, for he will save his people from their sins." All that will not fit in the stained glass window, of course, so there is just the beginning of it, set in glass the color of the moon: "Joseph, son of David, do not be afraid...."

The salutation is important. If the Messiah is to be born the son of David, then this is the man he must be born to. The prophets said so, and Matthew goes to great lengths to persuade us that what the prophets foresaw has come to pass. So that is it for Matthew: the annunciation to Joseph. There is no Mary in the picture at all, no lily, no *Magnificat*, no "Let it be to me according to your word." Mary has no lines at all, and while that significant omission makes some modern readers mad, it is no excuse for ignoring Joseph, who has his own part to play in the drama of divine birth.

According to Matthew, the whole grand experiment hangs on what happens with Joseph. If Joseph believes the angel, everything is on. The story can continue. Mary will have a home and a family and her child will be born the son of David. But if Joseph does not believe, then everything grinds to a halt. If he wakes up from his dream, shakes his head, and goes on to the courthouse to file the divorce papers, then Mary is an outcast forever—either killed by her family for disgracing them and herself or disowned by them and left to scratch out her living however she can, feeding herself and her illegitimate child on whatever she can beg or steal.

The child is Joseph's until he says otherwise. Whether or not his own seed is involved, he becomes the child's father the moment he says so, because the issue at stake is not a biological one but a legal one. "If someone says, 'This is my son,' he is so attested," reads Jewish law. Will Joseph claim the child or not? Will he believe the impossible and give it a home or will he stick with what makes sense and let the miracle go hungry?

According to Matthew, Joseph's belief is as crucial to the story as Mary's womb. God and all the angels are on her side, but it takes both parents to give birth to this remarkable child: Mary to give him life, and Joseph to give him a name: Jesus, son of David, from whose house the Messiah shall come.

In our own age of people who raise children without benefit of marriage, the issue of legitimacy sounds a bit quaint, but the heart of this story is much bigger and more profound than that. The heart of the story is about a just man who wakes up one day to find his life wrecked: his wife pregnant, his trust betrayed, his name ruined, his future revoked. It is about a righteous man who surveys a mess he has had absolutely nothing to do with and decides to believe that God is present in it. With every reason to disown it all, to walk away from it in search of a cleaner, more controlled life with an easier, more conventional wife, Joseph does not do that. He claims the scandal and gives it his name. He owns the mess—he legitimates it—and the mess becomes the place where the Messiah is born.

Do I need to say more? That quiet, old, peripheral man— the one with the missing sock and the candle wax on his sleeve—he is the one to watch. He is the one in the story who is most like us, presented day by day by day with circumstances beyond our control, with lives we would never have chosen for ourselves, tempted to divorce ourselves from it all when an angel whispers in our ears: "Do not fear. God is here. It may not be the life you had planned, but God may be born here too, if you will permit it."

That "if" is the real shocker—that God's "yes" depends on our own, that God's birth requires human partners—a Mary, a Joseph, a you, and a me—willing to believe the impossible, willing to claim the scandal, to adopt it and give it our names, accepting the whole sticky mess and rocking it in our arms. Our lives, our losses, our Lord. And not just each of us alone but the whole church of God, surveying a world that seems to have run amuck and proclaiming over and over again to anyone who will hear that God is still with us, that God is still being born in the mess and through it, within and among those who will still believe what angels tell them in their dreams.

"When Joseph awoke from sleep, he did as the angel of the Lord commanded him; he took her as his wife, but knew her not until she had borne a son; and he named him Jesus."

Laboring in Vain

It is too light a thing that you should be my servant to raise up the tribes of Jacob and to restore the survivors of Israel; I will give you as a light to the nations, that my salvation may reach to the end of the earth. (Isaiah 49:6)

NO ONE KNOWS for sure who this "servant" was. Isaiah had a way of getting so wrapped up in what God was giving him to say that he all but lost track of who he was. Like an actor who loves the play he is in so much that he can recite every line of it, Isaiah jumps from part to part. Sometimes when he says "I" he is speaking for himself. Sometimes he is speaking for God. And more than once, he speaks for an unidentified servant of God, someone who was chosen by God and who suffered for it.

Those of us who know Jesus think it sounds for all the world like him—a man of sorrows and acquainted with grief—but Isaiah also calls him Israel, without telling us whether he means one person named Israel or the whole nation. When we come upon the servant in the forty-ninth chapter of Isaiah, he is in deep despair. Nothing is working out for him. Everything he touches breaks. He knows that God has called him from his mother's womb; he knows that he is God's child, but that only intensifies his grief because he is convinced he has wasted his gifts. God has made his mouth like a sharp sword, but his words do not seem to be able to cut through anything. God has made him like a polished arrow, but he cannot seem to hit the target, let alone the mark. "I have labored in vain," he says, "I have spent my strength for nothing and vanity."

In the end, it does not matter whether we can name the person Isaiah paints for us, because the portrait already has a name. "God's Servant," it says, and that is enough. This is God's Chosen One, and whether the words are capitalized or not, they speak to all of us who are God's servants in this world. Whether we like it or not, every one of us is a full-fledged deputy of God's kingdom. Some of us are better at it than others and some of us do more harm than good, but none of us is excused. The moment we were baptized as Christ's own forever, we were set apart as God's servants in this world, and the very fact that we are still hanging around means that we have not resigned yet.

Whether we go to church because we believe or because we want to believe, we know that God has the power to change our lives and that people expect us to be different somehow—kinder and more generous, wiser and more honest. All of you with church stickers on your cars know what I mean. No more pulling in front of people or parking in spaces reserved for the handicapped. No more tailgating or coasting through stop signs. You have to let the other person go first, and you had better wash your car while you are at it, because you do not want people thinking Christians are slobs.

You get the idea. You are God's people, and God's people are called to be extraordinary: extra thoughtful, extra friendly, extra involved. So you are. You do and do and do. You volunteer, you join, you serve, you listen, you give. You leave home early in the morning and come home late at night. You take on other people's problems, you put them first, you invite them into your home. They try to take your coat and you give them your shirt as well.

You burn your candle at both ends, discovering that the reward for a job well done is not less work but more work, none of which stays done. You begin to wonder whether it is God you are serving or only your own ego. You snap at someone who does not deserve it and your bitterness surprises you. You start getting tired earlier and earlier in the day until finally one morning you cannot get out of bed at all. "I have labored in vain," you say to the ceiling. "I have spent my strength for nothing and vanity."

I expect that Isaiah's servant was feeling something like that when he confessed his own failure to God. Expecting to be fired or at least retired and replaced by someone more equal to the task, he tells God that he has accomplished nothing, is nothing, deserves nothing, but God does not accept his resignation. God—whose ideas of success and failure have never coincided with our own—has a better idea. "I will give you as a light to the nations," God says, "that my salvation may reach to the end of the earth."

Now that is divine logic for you. Fail at a large task and you are given a larger one. Produce hardly a spark in your own small corner of the world and you are promoted to light the whole planet. It is either a case of divine irony or else God knows something we servants do not know, namely, that our success does not depend on those who are chosen but on the one who chooses them, the Holy One of Israel, in whose hand the sharp sword cannot fail to dazzle, in whose bow the polished arrow cannot fail to find its mark.

The only way we can *truly* fail, apparently, is to remove ourselves from those hands, to let our own poor judgment make us quit our relationship with the Chooser, disqualifying ourselves from God's service on the grounds that our efforts are not good enough, our skills are not fine enough, our scores are not high enough. Who do we think we are?

When our own ideas of success go bankrupt, when our own notions of servanthood are exhausted, only then is there room for God to give us a new vision of ourselves. For Isaiah's servant, that vision was one of light—of epiphany—of being set on fire as God's beacon in the world. He had thought it was enough for him to do his duty, to do the particular tasks God had set before him, tasks at which he labored and labored until he had no strength left. He came to the end of his rope. He admitted defeat, and that is when God had some room to negotiate.

"Stop doing a job," God said. "Start being a light. Stop doing your duty. Start being mine. Stop worrying about whether or not you have done a good job. Start leaving that up to me. You can't see it the way I can. You just let your light shine and let me take care of the rest. I chose you and I've got good taste. I made you and I can be trusted."

That is not an authorized translation, mind you, but what if? What if the real test of our success as God's servants is not what we do but how we do it? What if the real measure of our extraordinariness as Christians is not our thoughtfulness or our friendliness or our busyness but our *spark*? What if the real sign of our witness to the light is not how much we accomplish but our own *lightness*, our own *reflection* of the bright God who has chosen us and lit us up and sent us into the world like candles into a dark room?

It is just an idea, but if there is anything to it then there is no such thing as laboring in vain. How would we know? Can a flame see its own light? Who asked our opinion? Who put us in charge? The Holy One of Israel has chosen us, has called us from our mothers' wombs and named our names, giving us mouths like sharp swords, making us like polished arrows. It is not up to us to decide whether we have succeeded or failed. It is not up to us to decide if we have labored in vain.

To spend our strength doing *that* is to spend it on nothing and vanity, while the call of God hauls so much more strenuously at our hearts, calling us to serve, certainly, but calling us first and last to stay as close as we know how to the one who has chosen us, to stay as close to the light as we can, so that our witness is not a matter of performing tasks or playing roles or meeting expectations but of remaining in white hot relationship with the one who is able to make epiphanies out of all our days.

It is just an idea, but if there is anything to it then it is too light a thing, you servants of God, that you should spend your strength doing your duty when what you have been called to do is to ignite, enflame, combust, burn, *shine* with the glory of the God who has chosen you, and given you to the world, bright lights to the end of the earth.